Historic Michigan Travel Guide - 8th Edition

HISTORIC MICHIGAN TRAVEL GUIDE

THE GUIDE TO HISTORICAL DESTINATIONS IN MICHIGAN

SPONSORED BY

meijer®

8th Edition

Edited by
Larry J. Wagenaar
and Amy Bradfield

Published by
The Historical Society of Michigan
7435 Westshire Dr.
Lansing, MI 48917
hsmichigan.org

Manufactured and printed in the United States of America.

ISBN 978-1-880311-15-8

TABLE OF CONTENTS

INTRODUCTION

Explore Michigan history!

The Historical Society of Michigan is proud to present this 8th Edition of the *Historic Michigan Travel Guide*. From the publication's humble beginnings in the 1970s as a small, hand-stapled publication, this travel guide has grown to be one of the largest printings of any book focused on Michigan's history.

Melding a love of travel with a passion for the past, this book will help you discover places you never knew existed along with sites you may have visited before that could use another look. Most of our state's history is preserved in these local museums, libraries, and historic sites, making many of them a must-see stop to get the true flavor of each community no matter where you are travelling in the Great Lakes State. You will find in these pages nearly 500 historical museums, sites, and attractions that allow you to experience the state's rich cultural and heritage resources like never before.

The *Historic Michigan Travel Guide* is divided by regions. Within each section, sites are listed alphabetically by the city or town name. You may also search for sites and cities using the index in the back of the book. All our member organizations were given the opportunity to refresh their information so that you would have the most up-to-date details to plan your trips. If we did not get a response from a member, we revised the data using websites and other sources. However, we recommend contacting the sites ahead of your visit for the latest information.

Each of the following destinations is operated by a member organization of the Historical Society of Michigan (HSM), which is a requirement to be included in this publication. The sites also need to have a physical location open to the public and be considered a "tourist attraction" of historical interest. If your local institution or one you visit is not included, it likely means we are unaware of it, or it is not an HSM member.

We hope using this book will take you on new journeys and help you gain a deeper understanding of the Great Lakes State's colorful past.

New to the Historical Society of Michigan?
The Historical Society of Michigan hosts exciting events, programs, and more. Learn more at *hsmichigan.org*.

ACKNOWLEDGEMENTS

This edition of the *Historic Michigan Travel Guide* could not have come together without the help of our sponsors, staff members, and Board of Trustees. Likewise, we greatly appreciate the hundreds of organizations that submitted information to the Historical Society of Michigan for inclusion.

I would like to thank my co-editor, Amy Bradfield, for all the hard work and many hours she put into developing this guide, which serves to promote cultural and heritage tourism in Michigan. We built on the work of previous editions to create this new volume, and many improvements were made to the design to make this the best *Historic Michigan Travel Guide* yet. We encourage you to use the QR codes listed for most entries, which can be scanned with a smartphone and will link you to the sites' web presence, to view current information about hours of operation.

I would also like to thank Meijer for serving as our sponsor. That help made it possible to do the extensive work of collecting the necessary data and writing, editing, typesetting, and publishing this guide. In addition, Meijer has provided distribution in all of its Michigan stores to make this new edition of the *Historic Michigan Travel Guide* widely available.

A special word of thanks goes to Amy Wagenaar for the design of the guide and compiling the information for this publication. The following staff members played a part in completing this guide: Erika McDowell, Shelby Laupp, Carolyn Niehaus, James Hall, Kathy Wollensak, Claire Herhold, Kim Loftus, Rachel Higginbotham, and Terri Assaf. In addition, I'd like to thank Deborah Larsen for proofreading this publication.

Larry J. Wagenaar
Executive Director and CEO, Historical Society of Michigan
Publisher, HSM Publications

WESTERN REGION

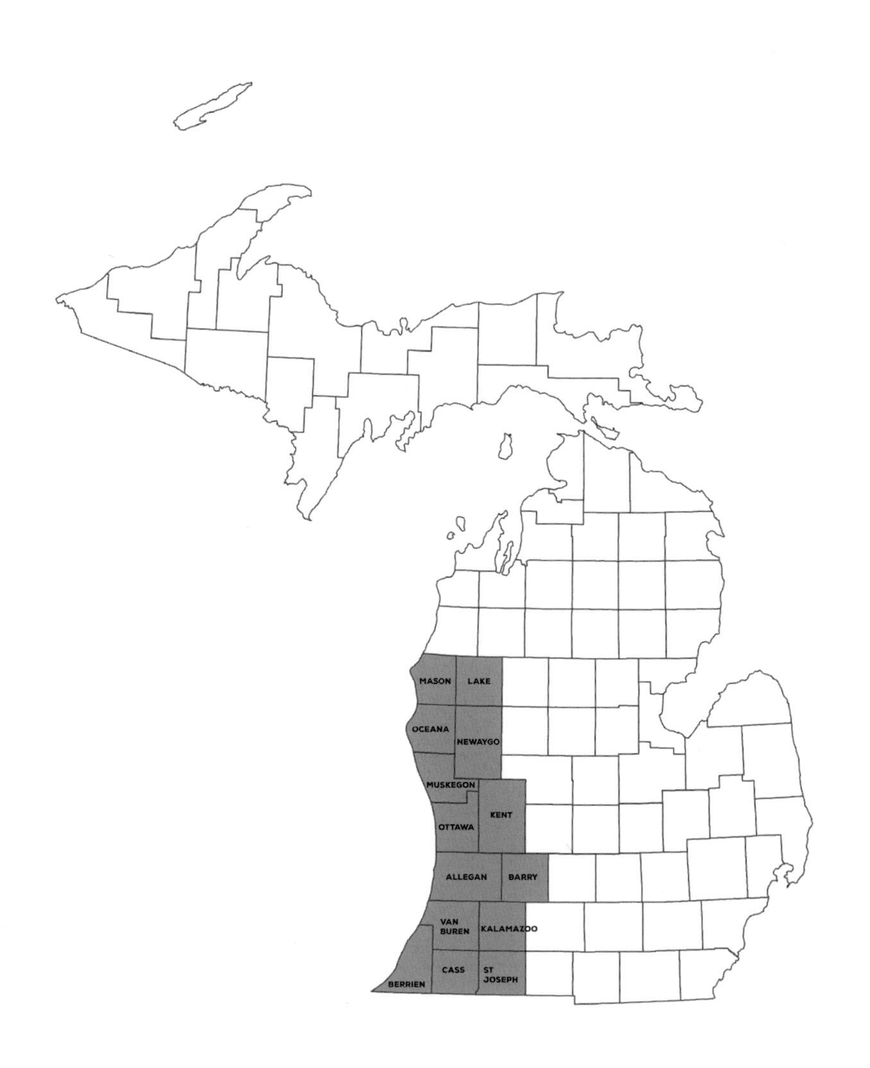

ADA

Ada History Center

ADDRESS: 7144 Headley St., Ada, MI 49301
ADMISSION: Free. Donations accepted.
ACCESSIBILITY: Fully accessible.
DESCRIPTION: The Ada History Center is home to the Averill Historical Museum—a turn-of-the-century farmhouse and barn—and the Ada Historical Society. Highlighting the unique history of the Ada community, the museum has permanent exhibits on the fur trade, life on the Thornapple and Grand Rivers, the railroad, area businesses, and more.
URL: *www.adahistorycenter.org*
CONTACT: AdaHistoricalSociety@gmail.com • (616) 676-9346

ALLEGAN

Allegan Old Jail Museum

ADDRESS: 113 Walnut St., Allegan, MI 49010
ADMISSION: Free. Donations accepted.
ACCESSIBILITY: Contact site.
DESCRIPTION: In 1963, the Allegan County Historical Society acquired the former jail, built in 1906, and converted it into the Old Jail Museum with period rooms and displays. Exhibits contain items from the pioneer days up to 1950 and include artifacts from the War of 1812, Civil War, Spanish American War, World War I, and World War II.
URL: *www.alleganoldjail.com*
CONTACT: oldjailmuseum06@yahoo.com • (269) 673-8292

John C. Pahl Historical Village

ADDRESS: 150 Allegan County Fair Dr., Allegan, MI 49010
ADMISSION: Free. Donations accepted.
ACCESSIBILITY: Fully accessible.
DESCRIPTION: The John C. Pahl Historical Village hosts several historical buildings, which were relocated from throughout the county. The buildings include the Jewett School, a one-room schoolhouse that holds classes during the week of the fair; a working blacksmith shop; and an authentically restored 1924 Chesapeake & Ohio wooden caboose.
URL: *www.alleganoldjail.com*
CONTACT: oldjailmuseum06@yahoo.com • (269) 673-8292

ALTO

Bowne Township Historical Museum

ADDRESS: 8240 Alden Nash, Alto, MI 49302
ADMISSION: Contact site.
ACCESSIBILITY: Partially accessible.
DESCRIPTION: Visitors to the museum will see artifacts from the mid-1800s through the 1900s from home to business to military. The Bowne Center School House is filled with old desks, books, and other school artifacts and historical information. The school is located on the southeast corner of 84th Avenue and Alden Nash Road.
URL: *Facebook: Bowne Township Historical Commission*
CONTACT: srjohnson4@charter.net • (616) 868-6424

BALDWIN

Lake County Historical Museum

ADDRESS: 915 N Michigan Ave., Baldwin, MI 49304
ADMISSION: Contact site.
ACCESSIBILITY: Fully accessible.
DESCRIPTION: Seven rooms of exhibits cover logging, Civilian Conservation Corps, Idlewild, tourism, youth camps, local businesses, and more. Several displays include hands-on participation. These exhibits rotate on a six-month basis so there is always something new. A research library includes over 8,000 scanned images, plat maps, family histories, yearbooks, and more.
URL: *Facebook: Lake County Historical Museum*
CONTACT: lakecountyhistory@hotmail.com • (231) 898-6500

BANGOR

Bangor Historical Society Museum

ADDRESS: 229 W. Monroe St., Bangor, MI 49013
ADMISSION: Contact site.
ACCESSIBILITY: Fully accessible.
DESCRIPTION: The Bangor Historical Society Museum is almost entirely about the history of Bangor. The museum contains a stuffed animal exhibit, various military uniforms, interesting signs from the community, and a Kalamazoo Toy Train toy exhibit with a G gauge track made in Bangor.
URL: *www.bangormihistory.com*
CONTACT: bangorhistoricalsociety@gmail.com • (269) 427-0611

BELMONT

Hyser Museum

ADDRESS: 6440 West River Dr., NE Belmont, MI 49306
ADMISSION: Contact site.
ACCESSIBILITY: Partially accessible.
DESCRIPTION: The Hyser Museum is located in the 1852 Greek Revival home of Dr. William Hyser, a pioneer surgeon and Civil War captain. It displays family living quarters, township artifacts, and is one of the last remaining structures of the original Plainfield Village. The museum is maintained by the Plainfield Grand Rogue Historical Society.
URL: *Facebook: Hyser Rivers Museum*
CONTACT: plainfieldhistory@gmail.com • (616) 644-1488

BENTON HARBOR

Morton House Museum

ADDRESS: 501 Territorial Rd., Benton Harbor, MI 49022
ADMISSION: Charge.
ACCESSIBILITY: Contact site.
DESCRIPTION: The Morton House, built in 1849, is the oldest house in the city of Benton Harbor. The Morton House Museum uses the Mortons and their home to fulfill their mission to be "The Home of Benton Harbor History." Yearly exhibits, books, and artifacts help to tell the story of Benton Harbor from its founding to today.
URL: *www.mortonhousemuseum.org*
CONTACT: bhmortonhouse@gmail.com • (269) 313-2106

BERRIEN SPRINGS

History Center at Courthouse Square

ADDRESS: 313 N. Cass St., Berrien Springs, MI 49103
ADMISSION: Free. Donations accepted.
ACCESSIBILITY: Partially accessible.
DESCRIPTION: The Berrien County Historical Association was established in 1968 to preserve the 1839 County Courthouse and serve as the heart of Berrien County's past. Renamed the History Center at Courthouse Square in 2014, the site offers permanent and temporary exhibits along with a robust calendar of events exploring the history, heritage, and culture of Berrien County.
URL: *www.berrienhistory.org*
CONTACT: Info@berrienhistory.org • (269) 471-1202

BUCHANAN

Pears Mill

ADDRESS: 121 South Oak St., Buchanan, MI 49107
ADMISSION: Contact site.
ACCESSIBILITY: Partially accessible.
DESCRIPTION: Pears Mill is an operational 1850s-era water-powered grist mill. Watching the sluice, waterwheel, powertrain, and millstones in action is fascinating and educational. Pears Mill also houses many historical grain milling artifacts. There is also a permanent exhibition of historical mercantile signs from Buchanan's Main Street retail district.
URL: *www.preservebuchanan.org*
CONTACT: preservebuchanan@gmail.com • (269) 235-9069

BYRON CENTER

Byron Area Historical Museum

ADDRESS: 2506 Prescott St., SW Byron Center, MI 49315
ADMISSION: Contact site.
ACCESSIBILITY: Fully accessible.
DESCRIPTION: The Byron Area Historical Museum includes an old two-story Town Hall. The upper level contains a military room and usable school room. Downstairs has exhibits on farming, a general store, and a large room of local family genealogy. It includes mastodon bones that were found in the area in 2017.
URL: *www.byroncentermuseum.com*
CONTACT: byronmuseum@sbcglobal.net • (616) 878-0888

CANNONSBURG

Cannon Township Historical Society & Museum

ADDRESS: 8045 Cannonsburg Rd., Cannonsburg, MI 49317
ADMISSION: Free. Donations accepted.
ACCESSIBILITY: Fully accessible.
DESCRIPTION: Cannon Township Historical Society & Museum houses Cannon Township artifacts, including school and family photographs. Visitors can also view machinery, furniture, household goods, and access a local genealogy collection. Please contact the site before visiting.
URL: *No website.*
CONTACT: (616) 874-7517

CASSOPOLIS

Pioneer Log Cabin Museum

ADDRESS: 400 South Broadway St., Cassopolis, MI 49031
ADMISSION: Free. Donations accepted.
ACCESSIBILITY: Contact site.
DESCRIPTION: The pioneer log cabin was built in 1923 from logs donated by descendants of early pioneers. The museum contains old tools, dollhouses, a bird collection, household items, a Civil War collection, and many other items related to the early history of Cass County. It is located in Shoestring Park, which overlooks Stone Lake.
URL: *Facebook: Pioneer Log Cabin Museum*
CONTACT: mpioneer1@aol.com • (269) 445-3759

Bogue House

ADDRESS: 20283 M-60, Cassopolis, MI 49031
ADMISSION: Free. Donations accepted.
ACCESSIBILITY: Contact site.
DESCRIPTION: The Bogue House was built around 1830 by Quaker abolitionists and Underground Railroad stationmasters Stephen and Hannah Bogue. They sheltered freedom seekers and started the Anti-Slavery Society in 1843. Visitors can walk in the attic where freedom seekers were hidden and learn how the house figured in the 1847 Kentucky Slave Raid.
URL: *www.urscc.org*
CONTACT: info@urscc.org • (269) 646-0401

Edward Lowe Foundation

ADDRESS: 58220 Decatur Rd., Cassopolis, MI 49031
ADMISSION: Free. Donations accepted.
ACCESSIBILITY: Fully accessible.
DESCRIPTION: The Edward Lowe Foundation was launched in 1985 by Ed and Darlene Lowe. Ed invented Kitty Litter in 1947, creating not only a new product, but also an entirely new industry. The foundation spotlights Lowe's business ventures and Big Rock Valley, the foundation's campus. Exhibits include video, print materials, photos, and artifacts dating back to the 1940s.
URL: *www.edwardlowe.org*
CONTACT: info@lowe.org • (800) 232-5693

CEDAR SPRINGS

Cedar Springs Historical Society & Museum

ADDRESS: 60 Cedar St., Cedar Springs, MI 49319
ADMISSION: Contact site.
ACCESSIBILITY: Fully accessible.
DESCRIPTION: Step back in time at the Cedar Springs Museum, where visitors can tour the Payne One-Room Schoolhouse, a turn-of-the-century home, the old general store, as well as find displays on Native-American history, lumbering, farming, and railroads. Also offered are genealogy assistance, microfilm access, 1800s-1900s maps and plat books, and research services.
URL: *www.cedarspringsmuseum.org*
CONTACT: cedarspringsmuseum@gmail.com • (616) 696-3335

COLOMA

North Berrien Historical Museum

ADDRESS: 300 Coloma Ave., Coloma, MI 49038
ADMISSION: Free. Donations accepted.
ACCESSIBILITY: Fully accessible.
DESCRIPTION: The museum focuses on the history of northern Berrien County and includes five buildings. The main gallery features Native-American history, lake resorts, rural schools, shipwrecks, daily life, and businesses, such as the Watervliet Paper Mill. The Nichols-Beverly Barn presents lumbering and agricultural history with the permanent exhibit "Moving from Forest to Fruit Belt."
URL: *www.northberrienhistory.org*
CONTACT: info@northberrienhistory.org • (269) 468-3330

COMSTOCK PARK

Alpine Township Historical Museum

ADDRESS: 5255 Alpine Ave. NW, Comstock Park, MI 49321
ADMISSION: Contact site.
ACCESSIBILITY: Fully accessible.
DESCRIPTION: The Alpine Township Historical Museum is located in the 1860 township hall, which was restored in 1987. Collections include photo galleries of early settlers, 12 one-room schools, and more than 300 township veterans. Visitors can also view furniture and artifacts of pioneer families and an extensive file of township family histories and obituaries.
URL: *www.alpinetwp.org*
CONTACT: raceder@comcast.net • (616) 784-1262

COOPERSVILLE

Coopersville Historical Museum

ADDRESS: 363 Main St., Coopersville, MI 49404
ADMISSION: Free. Donations accepted.
ACCESSIBILITY: Fully accessible.
DESCRIPTION: The museum's main red-brick building houses extensive railroad displays, along with early business, household, and military exhibits. The museum also houses memorabilia on Coopersville rock-and-roll star Del Shannon. The Sawmill & Early Settlers building commemorates pioneers of the area with a sawmill, model railroad, tools, logging items, and schoolroom.
URL: *www.coopersvillehistory.org*
CONTACT: budphoto@allcom.net • (616) 997-7240

Coopersville & Marne Railway

ADDRESS: 306 Main St., Coopersville, Michigan 49404
ADMISSION: Charge.
ACCESSIBILITY: Contact site.
DESCRIPTION: All aboard on the Coopersville and Marne Railway! Our vintage train travels between the city of Coopersville and the village of Marne, following seven miles of track originally built in 1858. Sit back, relax, and enjoy a bygone era of travel. On most trains, musicians and actors get passengers involved in the fun during our 90-minute trip back in time.
URL: *www.mitrain.net*
CONTACT: info@mitrain.net • (616) 997-7000

DELTON

Bernard Historical Museum

ADDRESS: 7135 West Delton Rd., Delton, MI 49046
ADMISSION: Free. Donations accepted.
ACCESSIBILITY: Fully accessible.
DESCRIPTION: The Bernard Historical Society was organized in 1962 based on the historical collection owned by Dr. Prosper Bernard. The collection of more than 40,000 artifacts dates from prehistoric times to the 1940s. The society also maintains a former hospital, 1873 Brown School, farm implement building, general store, seamstress building, and blacksmith shop.
URL: *www.bernardmuseum.org*
CONTACT: museumbernard@gmail.com • (269) 623-3565

DOUGLAS

History Center in Douglas

ADDRESS: 130 Center St., Douglas, MI 49406
ADMISSION: Contact site.
ACCESSIBILITY: Fully accessible.
DESCRIPTION: Housed in the 1866 Douglas Union School, the History Center in Douglas includes rotating exhibits, an art gallery, a Back-in-Time school experience, an archives and research center, and thematic learning stations on the 1.16-acre schoolhouse grounds. Visitors can also view a SuperMap in the Map Room Exhibit and enjoy various programs throughout the year.
URL: *www.mysdhistory.org*
CONTACT: director@mysdhistory.org • (269) 857-5751

DOWAGIAC

Dowagiac Area History Museum

ADDRESS: 201 East Division St., Dowagiac, MI 49047
ADMISSION: Free. Donations accepted.
ACCESSIBILITY: Fully accessible.
DESCRIPTION: The museum features 6,000 square feet of history in an updated facility. Highlights include exhibits on the Round Oak Stove Company, Heddon fishing tackle, the First Spaceman—Captain Iven C. Kincheloe, the Underground Railroad, and other local history. A temporary exhibit gallery rotates displays several times per year.
URL: *www.dowagiacmuseum.info*
CONTACT: info@dowagiacmuseum.info • (269) 783-2560

Heddon Museum

ADDRESS: 115 S. Front St., Dowagiac, MI 49047
ADMISSION: Free. Donations accepted.
ACCESSIBILITY: Fully accessible.
DESCRIPTION: Located in downtown Dowagiac, the Heddon Museum has all things related to the Heddon Fishing Tackle Company. More than 3,000 square feet of exhibit space explores the Heddon family, the iconic fishing tackle made by the largest tackle company in the world for several decades, and World War II production—as well as Heddon aviation and the Heddon truck.
URL: *www.heddon.dowagiacmuseum.info*
CONTACT: sarseneau@dowagiac.org • (269) 783-2560

EAST GRAND RAPIDS

East Grand Rapids History Room

ADDRESS: 956 Lakeside Dr. SE East, Grand Rapids, MI 49506
ADMISSION: Free. Donations accepted.
ACCESSIBILITY: Contact site.
DESCRIPTION: The primary purpose of the East Grand Rapids History Room is to obtain, preserve, and display artifacts related to the rich history of the area, including such topics as Reeds Lake and Ramona Park. The room is located on the upper level of the East Grand Rapids Branch, which is part of the Kent District Library system.

URL: *www.eastgr.org/569/East-Grand-Rapids-History-Room*
CONTACT: egrhistoryroom@gmail.com • (616) 241-2092

EDWARDSBURG

Edwardsburg Area Historical Museum

ADDRESS: 26818 Main St., Edwardsburg, MI 49112
ADMISSION: Free. Donations accepted.
ACCESSIBILITY: Fully accessible.
DESCRIPTION: The museum is located in an old house that once was a hotel. Visitors can view exhibits of historical items and photographs of area businesses, lakes, farms, railroads, churches, military uniforms, clocks, quilts, and schools as well as an area of "Growing Up In Edwardsburg." A collection of household goods depicts life of early settlers.

URL: *www.edwardsburgmuseum.org*
CONTACT: edwardsburgmuseum@yahoo.com • (269) 663-3005

FREMONT

Terry Wantz Historical Research Center

ADDRESS: 30 East Main St., Fremont, MI 49412
ADMISSION: Free. Donations accepted.
ACCESSIBILITY: Partially accessible.
DESCRIPTION: The Terry Wantz Historical Research Center offers family history research assistance and a local history collection—including historical photographs, documents, books, and artifacts. Visitors can browse our collection, use our online genealogical resources, receive help researching their families, or learn how to do genealogy themselves.

URL: *www.twhistoricalresearchcenter.com*
CONTACT: twhrc.info@gmail.com • (231) 335-2221

GRAND HAVEN

Midwest Miniatures Museum

ADDRESS: 20 S. 5th St., Grand Haven, MI 49417
ADMISSION: Charge.
ACCESSIBILITY: Fully accessible.
DESCRIPTION: The Midwest Miniatures Museum includes dozens of historical, miniature rooms and houses that seem to be awaiting their occupants' return. All are painstakingly created by artisans in 1:12 scale. The place settings are real crystal, silver, and hand-painted china. Some of the rooms even have light fixtures that brighten the displays.

URL: *www.midwestminiaturesmuseum.com*
CONTACT: info@midwestminiaturesmuseum.com • (616) 414-5809

Tri-Cities Historical Museum-Akeley Building

ADDRESS: 200 Washington Ave., Grand Haven, MI 49417
ADMISSION: Free. Donations accepted.
ACCESSIBILITY: Fully accessible.
DESCRIPTION: Exhibits tell the stories of Native Americans, early pioneers, lumberjacks, and French voyageurs. Victorian period rooms, medicine, agriculture, lumbering, maritime, tourism, and other exhibits portraying day-to-day lifestyles can be enjoyed by people of all ages and interests. The museum also includes temporary exhibits that change from time to time.
URL: *www.tri-citiesmuseum.org*
CONTACT: elayton@tchmuseum.org • (616) 842-0700

GRAND RAPIDS

Gerald R. Ford Presidential Museum

ADDRESS: 303 Pearl St. NW, Grand Rapids, MI 49504
ADMISSION: Charge.
ACCESSIBILITY: Fully accessible.
DESCRIPTION: At the core of the museum is the permanent exhibit, which allows visitors to experience highlights from President and Mrs. Ford's lives. The exhibit teaches democratic citizenship and allows for quiet reflection. In addition to the permanent exhibits, changing temporary exhibits draw artifacts from museums all over the country.
URL: *www.fordlibrarymuseum.gov*
CONTACT: ford.museum@nara.gov • (616) 254-0400

Grand Rapids Public Museum

ADDRESS: 272 Pearl St. NW, Grand Rapids, MI 49504
ADMISSION: Charge.
ACCESSIBILITY: Fully accessible.
DESCRIPTION: The Grand Rapids Public Museum is a place of never-ending inspiration and discovery, with a focus on science, history, and culture, and with three floors of hands-on fun and education exhibits for families to explore. Permanent exhibits include "Streets of Old Grand Rapids," "Anishinabek: The People of This Place," "Collecting A-Z," and the 1928 Spillman Carousel.
URL: *www.grpm.org*
CONTACT: info@grpm.org • (616) 929-1713

Heritage Hill Historic District

ADDRESS: 252 State St. SE, Suite 101 Grand Rapids, MI 49503
ADMISSION: Contact site.
ACCESSIBILITY: Contact site.
DESCRIPTION: Heritage Hill is a National, State, and Local Historic District near downtown Grand Rapids. It is one of Michigan's largest concentrations of nineteenth- and early- twentieth-century houses and includes nearly every style of American architecture from Greek Revival to Prairie. Home and garden tours are available during the year as well as self-guided walking tour maps.
URL: *www.heritagehillweb.org*
CONTACT: heritage@heritagehillweb.org • (616) 459-8950

Cascade Historical Society Museum

ADDRESS: 2865 Thornhills Ave., SE Grand Rapids, MI 49546
ADMISSION: Contact site.
ACCESSIBILITY: Fully accessible.
DESCRIPTION: The Cascade Historical Society preserves and records the history of Cascade Township. The museum was built in the nineteenth century, formally the township hall. The collections of the society include artifacts, photographs, newspaper clippings, journals, diaries, memorabilia, and limited exhibits.

URL: *www.cascadetwp.com*
CONTACT: vicsugoblu@comcast.net • (616) 676-9443

GRANDVILLE

Grandville Museum

ADDRESS: 3195 Wilson Ave. SW, Grandville, MI 49418
ADMISSION: Free. Donations accepted.
ACCESSIBILITY: Fully accessible.
DESCRIPTION: Located on the lower level of City Hall, the Grandville Historical Museum is operated and maintained by the Grandville Historical Commission. The museum's collection includes artifacts from the Grandville area such as home furnishings, office equipment, photographs, plat maps, yearbooks, obituaries, and a mastodon skeleton found in the area in the early 1980s.

URL: *www.cityofgrandville.com/our_community/museum.php*
CONTACT: grandvilleHC@hotmail.com • (616) 531-3030

HART

Chadwick-Munger House

ADDRESS: 114 Dryden St., Hart, MI 49420
ADMISSION: Free. Donations accepted.
ACCESSIBILITY: Partially accessible.
DESCRIPTION: The Chadwick-Munger House is the headquarters of the Oceana County Historical & Genealogical Society. It contains county newspapers, postcards of the area, historical background on the area's settlers, and genealogical history of many of the county residents.

URL: *www.oceanahistory.org*
CONTACT: info@oceanahistory.org • (231) 873-2600

Hart Historic District and Museum

ADDRESS: 570 E. Lincoln St., Hart, MI 49420
ADMISSION: Free. Donations accepted.
ACCESSIBILITY: Fully accessible.
DESCRIPTION: The Hart Historic District and Museum includes multiple restored buildings housing collections and displays that allow visitors to learn about and experience everyday life from 150 years ago. Some of the collections include antique tools, animated antique dolls, and pipe organ as well as a fire station, feed mill, and more.

URL: *www.harthistoricdistrict.com*
CONTACT: pharmleigh@gmail.com • (231) 873-7604

HARTFORD

VanBuren County Historical Museum

ADDRESS: 58471 Red Arrow Hwy., Hartford, MI 49057
ADMISSION: Charge.
ACCESSIBILITY: Fully accessible.
DESCRIPTION: The museum is housed in a former county poorhouse that was built circa 1884. The building features three floors of historical items and exhibits, including a one-room school, general store, music room, old-fashioned kitchen, turn-of-the-century parlor, old dentist office, and military room. There is also a replica log cabin and blacksmith workshop on the grounds.
URL: *Facebook: VanBuren County Historical Museum*
CONTACT: museum@vanburencountyhistoricalsociety.org • (269) 500-1450

HASTINGS

Historic Charlton Park Village & Museum

ADDRESS: 2545 S. Charlton Park Rd., Hastings, MI 49058
ADMISSION: Contact site.
ACCESSIBILITY: Partially accessible.
DESCRIPTION: The Historic Charlton Park Village and Museum offers many options for outdoor enthusiasts including hiking, boating, and swimming. Visit the turn-of-the-century historic village to explore more than 30,000 artifacts that represent agricultural equipment, vocational tools, furniture, textiles, housewares, firearms, communication devices, and archival documents.
URL: *www.charltonpark.org*
CONTACT: info@charltonpark.org • (269) 945-3775

HICKORY CORNERS

Gilmore Car Museum

ADDRESS: 6865 Hickory Rd., Hickory Corners, MI 49060
ADMISSION: Charge.
ACCESSIBILITY: Fully accessible.
DESCRIPTION: The 90-acre Gilmore Car Museum campus is home to nearly 400 incredible vehicles and 7 independent auto museums, all for one price. The site contains several historical buildings, including vintage car dealerships, a 1930s gas station, a small-town train depot, and an authentic 1940s diner that serves lunch. A vast collection of auto original artwork and advertising is also available.
URL: *www.gilmorecarmuseum.org*
CONTACT: info@gilmorecarmuseum.org • (269) 671-5089

HOLLAND

Holland Museum

ADDRESS: 31 W. 10th St., Holland, MI 49423
ADMISSION: Charge.
ACCESSIBILITY: Fully accessible.
DESCRIPTION: The museum features cultural attractions from the "old country," including Dutch paintings and exhibits from the Netherlands Pavilion of the 1939 New York World's Fair. Displays also highlight maritime and agricultural history. Artifacts include local historical items from the start of "Holland Kolonies" to locally produced furniture and automotive and boat-building components.
URL: *www.hollandmuseum.org*
CONTACT: hollandmuseum@hollandmuseum.org • (616) 796-3329

Cappon House

ADDRESS: 228 W. 9th St., Holland, MI 49423
ADMISSION: Charge.
ACCESSIBILITY: Partially accessible.
DESCRIPTION: The Italianate Cappon House was built by Holland's first mayor and tannery owner, Isaac Cappon, after the fire of 1871. Used by the family until 1980, the building has since been restored and furnished with Grand Rapids furniture.

URL: *www.hollandmuseum.org*
CONTACT: hollandmuseum@hollandmuseum.org • (616) 796-3329

Settlers House

ADDRESS: 190 W. 9th St., Holland, MI 49423
ADMISSION: Charge.
ACCESSIBILITY: Partially accessible.
DESCRIPTION: One of the few buildings to survive the Holland fire, the Settlers House was built in 1867 by Irish Canadian shipbuilder Thomas Morrissey. A series of working-class families lived in the home over the course of its long history.

URL: *www.hollandmuseum.org*
CONTACT: hollandmuseum@hollandmuseum.org • (616) 796-3329

Olive Township Museum

ADDRESS: 11768 Polk St., Holland, MI 49424
ADMISSION: Contact site.
ACCESSIBILITY: Fully accessible.
DESCRIPTION: The museum was formerly the Olive Center School, which housed grades K-8. There are many interesting items pertaining to Olive Township and the local community, including photographs, artifacts, and more. The Olive Township Historical Society also provides interactive maps via its website for the Pigeon River Quilt Trail in the Olive Township area.

URL: *www.olivetownship.org/oths*
CONTACT: info@olivetownship.org • (616) 786-9996

Pump House Museum

ADDRESS: 2282 Ottawa Beach Rd., Holland, MI 49424
ADMISSION: Free. Donations accepted.
ACCESSIBILITY: Fully accessible.
DESCRIPTION: The Pump House is the last surviving structure of the Hotel Ottawa complex and renovations began in the early 2010s to convert the building to a museum. Digital displays in the museum have information about the Big Red lighthouse, Lakewood Farm, and Jenison Electric Amusement Park. Exhibits are frequently changed, but all tell the story of the Ottawa Beach area.

URL: *www.historicottawabeachsociety.org*
CONTACT: info@historicottawabeachsociety.org • (616) 607-6854

Windmill Island Gardens

ADDRESS: 1 Lincoln Ave., Holland, MI 49423
ADMISSION: Charge.
ACCESSIBILITY: Partially accessible.
DESCRIPTION: Tour the authentic Dutch windmill that De Zwaan brought from the Netherlands in 1964. Enjoy Dutch architecture, horticulture, and floriculture. Dutch treasures include an Amsterdam street organ, antique Dutch carousel, Little Netherlands village, gift shop, and much more.

URL: *www.windmillisland.org*
CONTACT: windmill@cityofholland.com • (616) 355-1030

IDLEWILD

Idlewild Historic & Cultural Center

ADDRESS: 7025 Broadway Ave., Idlewild, MI 49642
ADMISSION: Free. Donations accepted.
ACCESSIBILITY: Fully accessible.
DESCRIPTION: Idlewild is a year-round, tranquil retreat. The forests beckon visitors with a promise of good hunting and the area's lakes provide the perfect setting for leisurely boating and other warm-weather pursuits. Visitors to the center will learn about the founders of Idlewild and the famous African Americans who made their summer homes and permanent residences in Lake County.

URL: *www.historicidlewild.org*
CONTACT: fivecap@fivecap.org • (231) 757-3785

JENISON

Jenison Historical Museum

ADDRESS: 28 Port Sheldon, Jenison, MI 49428
ADMISSION: Free. Donations accepted.
ACCESSIBILITY: Partially accessible.
DESCRIPTION: The Jenison Historical Museum, maintained by the Jenison Historical Association, is a place to learn about the heritage of Jenison and the surrounding Georgetown Township area. Historical artifacts on display include medical instruments, a working 5-foot cash register from the L&L Store, a Morning Glory Talking Machine, and period furnishings.

URL: *www.jenisonhistory.org*
CONTACT: info@jenisonhistory.org • (616) 457-4398

KALAMAZOO

Kalamazoo Valley Museum

ADDRESS: 230 North Rose St., Kalamazoo, MI 49007
ADMISSION: Free. Donations accepted.
ACCESSIBILITY: Fully accessible.
DESCRIPTION: Attractions include an interactive science gallery, a history gallery, a planetarium, a children's landscape preschool area, and national traveling exhibits. Also featured are 56,000 objects made or used in Southwest Michigan, along with samples of materials from other times and places. The museum offers a regional history collection and more than 20,000 images for researchers.

URL: *www.kalamazoomuseum.org*
CONTACT: museumstaff@kvcc.edu • (269) 373-7990

KENTWOOD

Heritage Room at the Richard L. Root Branch Library

ADDRESS: 4950 Breton Rd. SE, Kentwood, MI 49508
ADMISSION: Contact site.
ACCESSIBILITY: Fully accessible.
DESCRIPTION: The commission shares its history at the Richard L. Root Branch Library. Collections include artifacts, photographs, documents, and oral histories. The museum offers this history through educational programs, exhibits, displays, and other special events.
URL: *www.kentwood-historic.weebly.com*
CONTACT: golderl@ci.kentwood.mi.us • (616) 554-0709

LOWELL

Fallasburg Historical Society

ADDRESS: 13944 Covered Bridge Rd. NE, Lowell, MI 49331
ADMISSION: Contact site.
ACCESSIBILITY: Fully accessible.
DESCRIPTION: Fallasburg Village is a nationally and state designated historic district. The 42-acre site contains a schoolhouse, two vintage barns, three homesteads, and a cemetery. Fallasburg is also home to a covered bridge that is the only one of its kind in the area still open to automobile traffic.
URL: *www.fallasburg.org*
CONTACT: info@fallasburg.org • (616) 987-1150

Lowell Area Historical Museum

ADDRESS: 325 W. Main St., Lowell, MI 49331
ADMISSION: Charge.
ACCESSIBILITY: Fully accessible.
DESCRIPTION: The Lowell Area Historical Museum is housed in the historic Graham Building, built in 1873 as a residential duplex. Today, the building features period rooms, galleries dedicated to early Lowell history, business and industry, the fur trade, and a changing exhibit space. Historical signage throughout the community continues the story of the past.
URL: *www.lowellmuseum.org*
CONTACT: history@lowellmuseum.org • (616) 897-7688

LUDINGTON

Port of Ludington Maritime Museum

ADDRESS: 217 S. Lakeshore Dr., Ludington, MI 49431
ADMISSION: Charge.
ACCESSIBILITY: Fully accessible.
DESCRIPTION: The museum brings history to life with storytelling, displays, and interactive exhibits that entertain and inspire a deeper appreciation for the region's maritime history. Located in the former U.S. Coast Guard Station, this family-friendly, three-story museum overlooks Lake Michigan's wild shoreline, extending the maritime experience beyond its doors in this vacation wonderland.
URL: *www.ludingtonmaritimemuseum.org*
CONTACT: Contact via website. • (231) 425-3825

Historic White Pine Village

ADDRESS: 1687 S. Lakeshore Dr., Ludington, MI 49431
ADMISSION: Charge.
ACCESSIBILITY: Fully accessible.
DESCRIPTION: This site brings history to life with the late-nineteeth- to early-twentieth-century pioneer village. Boasting 30 historical exhibit buildings filled with artifacts depicting the history of the area, including the original 1849 Mason County Courthouse and an authentic steam locomotive. Visitors also interact with first-person reenactors of actual personages from Mason County.
URL: *www.historicwhitepinevillage.org*
CONTACT: Contact via website. • (231) 843-4808

Big Sable Point Lighthouse

ADDRESS: 8800 W M-116, Ludington, MI 49431
ADMISSION: Charge.
ACCESSIBILITY: Partially accessible.
DESCRIPTION: The Big Sable Point Lighthouse features its original keepers' quarters, which are attached to the tower. The quarters provide housing for the summer volunteers, a gift shop, and a video room for visitors. Visitors can also climb the 130 steps to the watchtower, walk out on the catwalk, and witness spectacular views of the Ludington State Park and Lake Michigan.
URL: *www.splka.org*
CONTACT: splkadirector@gmail.com • (231) 845-7417

Ludington North Breakwater Light

ADDRESS: Sterns Park Downtown Ludington, Ludington, MI 49431
ADMISSION: Charge.
ACCESSIBILITY: Contact site.
DESCRIPTION: The lighthouse is located on the north breakwater pier at the end of Main Street in Ludington. Each level has interesting items and pictures for visitors to explore as they make their way to the lantern room. At the top, guests are treated to a view of Ludington harbor.
URL: *www.splka.org*
CONTACT: splkadirector@gmail.com • (231) 845-7417

MEARS

Oceana Historical Park Museum Complex

ADDRESS: 5809 Fox Rd., Mears, MI 49436
ADMISSION: Free. Donations accepted.
ACCESSIBILITY: Fully accessible.
DESCRIPTION: The Oceana Historical Park Museum Complex located in Mears includes a variety of structures and displays that showcase the history of the area. The Swift Lathers home includes a tool museum that displays vintage tools from corn shellers to drill bits and the Transportation Museum includes boats, tractors, dune buggies and more.
URL: *www.oceanahistory.org*
CONTACT: info@oceanahistory.org • (231) 873-2600

Old Town Hall

ADDRESS: 5698 Fox Rd.,Mears, MI 49436
ADMISSION: Free. Donations accepted.
ACCESSIBILITY: Fully accessible.
DESCRIPTION: The Old Town Hall depicts a replica "country schoolroom." Visitors can view a one-room schoolhouse and explore other special exhibits that are changed annually. The Old Town Hall is maintained and operated by the Oceana County Historical & Genealogical Society, whose mission is to collect, preserve, and disseminate knowledge of the history of Oceana County.
URL: *www.oceanahistory.org*
CONTACT: info@oceanahistory.org • (231) 873-2600

Little Sable Point Lighthouse

ADDRESS: 287 North Lighthouse Dr., Mears, MI 49436
ADMISSION: Charge.
ACCESSIBILITY: Fully accessible.
DESCRIPTION: Burrowed amidst the Silver Lake sand dunes and evergreen forests stands the spectacular Little Sable Point Lighthouse. The 1874 natural brick tower at the base of Lake Michigan is 107 feet tall and still harboring its original third order Fresnel lens. Climb the tower to take in the magnificent views. Activity booklet for children with paid admission.
URL: *www.splka.org*
CONTACT: splkadirector@gmail.com • (231) 845-7417

MUSKEGON

Fire Barn Museum

ADDRESS: 510 W. Clay Ave., Muskegon, MI 49440
ADMISSION: Charge.
ACCESSIBILITY: Contact site.
DESCRIPTION: The museum showcases firefighting equipment from the 1880s to the present day. Built in 1976, the structure is modeled after Hackley Hose Company #2—an early fire station funded by Charles Hackley. The second floor hosts a vignette showing the sleeping quarters of the company's original firefighters. Fire-bucket brigades and other special activities are held during the summer.
URL: *www.lakeshoremuseum.org*
CONTACT: jackie@lakeshoremuseum.org • (231) 722-7578

Hackley & Hume Historic Site

ADDRESS: 484 W. Webster Ave., Muskegon, MI 49440
ADMISSION: Charge.
ACCESSIBILITY: Contact site.
DESCRIPTION: The Hackley & Hume Historic Site preserves the Victorian mansions of Muskegon's most well-known lumber barons. The homes—built in the late 1800s—feature period furnishings and unique architectural elements. The site also includes a museum store and the City Barn, which contains exhibits on Muskegon history.
URL: *www.lakeshoremuseum.org*
CONTACT: jackie@lakeshoremuseum.org • (231) 722-7578

Scolnik House of the Depression Era

ADDRESS: 504 W. Clay Ave., Muskegon, MI 49440
ADMISSION: Charge.
ACCESSIBILITY: Contact site.
DESCRIPTION: This house museum—part of the Lakeshore Museum Center—depicts a single-family home that was divided into two apartments during the Great Depression. From bedrolls to a party-line telephone, visitors are immersed in the 1930s. Tickets can be purchased at the Hackley & Hume Historic Site's City Barn.

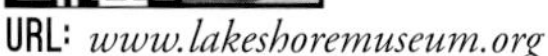

URL: *www.lakeshoremuseum.org*
CONTACT: jackie@lakeshoremuseum.org • (231) 722-7578

Muskegon Heritage Museum of Business & Industry

ADDRESS: 561 W. Western Ave., Muskegon, MI 49440
ADMISSION: Charge.
ACCESSIBILITY: Fully accessible.
DESCRIPTION: The museum's collection includes informational exhibits, artifacts, and photos pertaining to Muskegon's industries, products, and business. The museum features a working steam engine with a line shaft that runs 11 machine tools. There is also a working Brunswick pinsetter, a spring winding machine, and over 80 other companies represented in exhibits.
URL: *www.lakeshoremuseum.org*
CONTACT: jackie@lakeshoremuseum.org • (231) 722-1363

Muskegon Museum of History & Science

ADDRESS: 430 W. Clay Ave., Muskegon, MI 49440
ADMISSION: Charge.
ACCESSIBILITY: Fully accessible.
DESCRIPTION: A tour of the museum offers visitors an opportunity to explore 400,000 million years of Michigan in the making and features a life-size mastodon. Mastodon bones found in nearby Rothbury are also on display. Visitors of all ages will enjoy hands-on fun in several museum galleries.
URL: *www.lakeshoremuseum.org*
CONTACT: melissa@lakeshoremuseum.org • (231) 722-0278

Muskegon Museum of Art

ADDRESS: 296 W. Webster Ave., Muskegon, MI 49440
ADMISSION: Charge.
ACCESSIBILITY: Fully accessible.
DESCRIPTION: Established in 1912, the museum is renowned for its permanent collection of American and European paintings, sculptures, prints, and drawings. Regularly on view are works by artists such as John Steuart Curry, Edward Hopper, and Winslow Homer. Additionally, the museum's studio glass collection is among the finest in the Midwest.
URL: *www.muskegonartmuseum.org*
CONTACT: khepler@muskegonartmuseum.org • (231) 720-2570

S.S. Milwaukee Clipper

ADDRESS: 2098 Lakeshore Dr., Muskegon, MI 49442
ADMISSION: Charge.
ACCESSIBILITY: Partially accessible.
DESCRIPTION: The S.S. *Milwaukee Clipper* is the oldest remaining passenger steamship on the Great Lakes. Complete with the original Quadruple Expansion steam engine and equipment, the 119-year-old, 361-foot ship is listed on the National Register of Historic Places. On guided tours, visitors will learn how people traveled on a steamboat in the twentieth century.
URL: *www.milwaukeeclipper.com*
CONTACT: milwaukeeclipper@gmail.com • (231) 299-0784

USS LST 393 Veterans Museum

ADDRESS: 560 Mart St., Muskegon, MI 49440
ADMISSION: Charge.
ACCESSIBILITY: Partially accessible.
DESCRIPTION: Visit a restored World War II USS *LST 393*—a 350-foot landing ship tank—and view artifacts from twentieth- and twenty-first-century wars and services. The museum honors all veterans from all branches of the American armed forces and provides educational programs for students and the general public.
URL: *www.lst393.org*
CONTACT: info@lst393.org • (231) 730-1477

USS Silversides Submarine Museum

ADDRESS: 1346 Bluff St., Muskegon, MI 49441
ADMISSION: Charge.
ACCESSIBILITY: Fully accessible.
DESCRIPTION: The USS *Silversides* Submarine Museum honors men and women of the United States military, preserves military history, and provides experiences that educate the public about past and present military history and technology. The museum has permanent and temporary exhibits and visitors can tour the USS *Silversides* Gato-class submarine and a U.S. Coast Guard cutter.
URL: *www.silversidesmuseum.org*
CONTACT: contactus@silversidesmuseum.org • (231) 755-1230

NEW BUFFALO

New Buffalo Railroad Museum

ADDRESS: 530 S. Whittaker St., New Buffalo, MI 49117
ADMISSION: Free. Donations accepted.
ACCESSIBILITY: Fully accessible.
DESCRIPTION: Located on the grounds of what was once the largest train yard in Southwest Michigan, the museum contains items recalling New Buffalo's proud heritage as a railroad hub for both the Pere Marquette and Chesapeake & Ohio lines. Visitors can stroll through the Chessie Box Car and Troop Pullman Sleeper Car as well as operate the hand-crafted model train layout.
URL: *www.new-buffalo-railroad-museum.org*
CONTACT: ask@newbuffalorailroadmuseum.org • (269) 820-1504

NEWAYGO

Heritage Museum of Newaygo County

ADDRESS: 12 Quarterline Rd., Newaygo, MI 49337
ADMISSION: Free. Donations accepted.
ACCESSIBILITY: Fully accessible.
DESCRIPTION: The Heritage Museum of Newaygo County offers a look into the unique history and heritage of the Lower Peninsula's largest county, including topics such as logging, farming, tourism, and Native Americans. In addition, unique works by local artists dot the public spaces of the newly renovated museum, located in Newaygo's historic downtown.
URL: *www.newaygocountyhistory.org*
CONTACT: sradtke@newaygocountyhistory.org • (231) 652-5003

NILES

Chapin Mansion

ADDRESS: 508 E. Main St., Niles, MI 49120
ADMISSION: Contact site.
ACCESSIBILITY: Partially accessible.
DESCRIPTION: Henry and Ruby Chapin constructed their home in 1882. Donated to the city of Niles in 1933, it served as the city hall and a hospital. Ornate stained-glass windows, beveled mirrors, impressive brass chandeliers, beautiful hand-carved woodwork, and nine fireplaces will transport you back to the ornate Aesthetic Movement of the 1880s.
URL: *www.nileshistorycenter.org*
CONTACT: nileshistory@nilesmi.org • (269) 845-4054

Fort St. Joseph Museum

ADDRESS: 508 E. Main St., Niles, MI 49120
ADMISSION: Free. Donations accepted.
ACCESSIBILITY: Partially accessible.
DESCRIPTION: Part of the Niles History Center, this museum is located in the former carriage house of the Chapin Mansion and features exhibits from the prehistoric era through the 1691 founding of Fort St. Joseph to the modern businesses and industrial era. Highlights include archaeological discoveries, pictographs drawn by Chief Sitting Bull, and interactive elements for children.
URL: *www.nileshistorycenter.org*
CONTACT: nileshistory@nilesmi.org • (269) 845-4054

OTSEGO

Otsego Area Historical Society Museum

ADDRESS: 218 N. Farmer St., Otsego, MI 49078
ADMISSION: Free. Donations accepted.
ACCESSIBILITY: Fully accessible.
DESCRIPTION: The society is dedicated to promoting the history of Otsego and its surroundings. We operate and maintain a museum housed in the historic Water Works building at the North Farmer Street bridge. The museum's displays showcase the town's local history and change periodically. Preservation projects feature Otsego's 100-year-old homes and historic paper mill industry.
URL: *www.otsegohistory.org*
CONTACT: oahs@otsegohistory.org • (269) 692-3775

PENTWATER

Pentwater Historical Museum

ADDRESS: 85 South Rutledge, Pentwater, MI 49449
ADMISSION: Free. Donations accepted.
ACCESSIBILITY: Fully accessible.
DESCRIPTION: The museum showcases the diverse history of the greater Pentwater Area, which was part of the nineteenth century's brickmaking, furniture-making, and lumbering industries. It also has displays on the area's rich maritime history. A map for a self-guided walking tour leads visitors to many older homes and buildings as well as the historical interpretive panels located through the village.
URL: *www.pentwaterhistoricalsociety.org*
CONTACT: info@pentwaterhistoricalsociety.org • (810) 577-6591

QUINCY

Quincy Historical Museum

ADDRESS: 10 E. Jefferson St., Quincy, MI 49082
ADMISSION: Contact site.
ACCESSIBILITY: Contact site.
DESCRIPTION: The museum, erected in 1874 by a Seventh Day Adventist congregation, is the only brick church in the village of Quincy and numbers among the oldest structures. With the efforts of community volunteers and the Quincy Historical Society, the building has been restored, the grounds improved, and displays created with the many donated artifacts and memorabilia.
URL: *www.quincy-mi.org*
CONTACT: khargreave@quincy-mi.org • (517) 639-4595

ROCKFORD

Algoma Township Historical Society

ADDRESS: 10531 Algoma Ave., Rockford, MI 49341
ADMISSION: Contact site.
ACCESSIBILITY: Partially accessible.
DESCRIPTION: Established in 1986, the Algoma Township Historical Society gathers and catalogs historical artifacts and archives for the purpose of displaying and preserving the history of the township. The society also publishes a quarterly newsletter and holds monthly meetings with special speakers and activities. Visitors can view artifacts in display cabinets at the Algoma Township Hall.
URL: *www.algomatwp.org*
CONTACT: juliesjogren@gmail.com • (616) 866-1583

Rockford Area Museum

ADDRESS: 21 South Monroe St., Rockford, MI 49341
ADMISSION: Free. Donations accepted.
ACCESSIBILITY: Fully accessible.
DESCRIPTION: The Rockford Area Historical Society has operated the RAM, Rockford Area Museum, since 1976. Exhibits focus on the development of the Rockford area as a logging community and its evolution into a dynamic small city. Other exhibits tell the story of Rockford's business community, schools, and connection to America's military history and agriculture.
URL: *www.rockfordmuseum.org*
CONTACT: rockfordmuseum@gmail.com • (616) 866-2235

SAUGATUCK

Saugatuck-Douglas History Museum

ADDRESS: 735 Park St., Saugatuck, MI 49453
ADMISSION: Free. Donations accepted.
ACCESSIBILITY: Fully accessible.
DESCRIPTION: Visitors to the Saugatuck-Douglas Museum can engage with interactive exhibits on the area's fascinating history, including an exhibit on the Saugatuck Gap Filler Annex—a local landmark known better as the Mount Baldhead radar. The museum's changing exhibits also feature regional art collections and historical maps and photographs.
URL: *www.mysdhistory.org*
CONTACT: director@mysdhistory.org • (269) 857-5751

SCHOOLCRAFT

Dr. Nathan Thomas Underground Railroad House

ADDRESS: 613 East Cass St., Schoolcraft, MI 49087
ADMISSION: Charge.
ACCESSIBILITY: Partially accessible.
DESCRIPTION: Schoolcraft's first physician, Dr. Nathan Thomas, reportedly opened his home to over 1,000 fugitive slaves as they passed through Southern Michigan on the Underground Railroad. The Underground Railroad House stands as a tribute to the courage of those who sought to escape slavery and those who gave aid. Tours available by appointment.
URL: *www.nps.gov/nr/travel/underground/mi1.htm*
CONTACT: schoolcrafthistorical@hotmail.com • (269) 679-4304

SOUTH HAVEN

Michigan Maritime Museum

ADDRESS: 260 Dyckman Ave., South Haven, MI 49090
ADMISSION: Charge.
ACCESSIBILITY: Partially accessible.
DESCRIPTION: Visit the museum's newly expanded waterfront campus in the heart of South Haven's maritime district. Explore multiple permanent and changing exhibits detailing the rich heritage of industry and recreation on Michigan's Great Lakes and waterways. Sail into history aboard a fleet of vessels in the summer and learn the traditional skills that keep them afloat in the winter.
URL: *www.michiganmaritimemuseum.org*
CONTACT: info@mimaritime.org • (269) 637-8078

Liberty Hyde Bailey Museum

ADDRESS: 903 S. Bailey Ave., South Haven, MI 49090
ADMISSION: Free. Donations accepted.
ACCESSIBILITY: Fully accessible.
DESCRIPTION: The Liberty Hyde Bailey Museum presents the stories of the Bailey family members' lives, loves, and adventures. It is situated in the childhood home of the "Father of Modern Horticulture," Dr. Liberty Hyde Bailey Jr. Built in 1858 by Liberty Hyde Bailey Sr., the museum is set in a park featuring themed gardens demonstrating aspects of Dr. Bailey's research.
URL: *www.libertyhydebailey.org*
CONTACT: info@libertyhydebailey.org • (269) 637-3251

Michigan Flywheelers Museum

ADDRESS: 06285 68th St., South Haven, MI 49090
ADMISSION: Charge.
ACCESSIBILITY: Partially accessible.
DESCRIPTION: The 80-acre, open-air Michigan Flywheelers Museum provides visitors the opportunity to learn about life as it was in early farming communities. A self-guided tour of the Old Towne includes stops at a blacksmith shop, sawmill, shingle mill, jail, and gas station. Open from Memorial Day to Labor Day, the museum also displays a collection of antique engines and tractors.
URL: *www.michiganflywheelers.org*
CONTACT: michiganflywheelers@yahoo.com • (269) 639-2010

SPARTA

Sparta Township Historical Commission

ADDRESS: 71 N Union St., Sparta, MI 49345
ADMISSION: Contact site.
ACCESSIBILITY: Fully accessible.
DESCRIPTION: The commission maintains two buildings: the Myers School Museum and the History Center. Visitors to the one-room schoolhouse can see textbooks, chalkboards, and desks from long ago. The History Center is located at 71 N Union St. in Sparta. The collection includes local maps, atlases, newspapers, obituaries, death certificates, and yearbooks.
URL: *www.spartahistory.org*
CONTACT: history@spartahistory.org • (616) 606-0765

SPRING LAKE

Dewitt School House

ADDRESS: 17716 Taft St., Spring Lake, MI 49456
ADMISSION: Free. Donations accepted.
ACCESSIBILITY: Contact site.
DESCRIPTION: The Dewitt School House presents a variety of classroom programs for children to allow them to experience what school and the community was like more than 100 years ago. Located in Spring Lake Township, the museum offers grade-specific tours or will work with groups to design an experience based on specific needs.
URL: *www.tri-citiesmuseum.org*
CONTACT: jbunke@tchmuseum.org • (616) 842-0700

ST. JOSEPH

Heritage Museum and Cultural Center

ADDRESS: 601 Main St., St. Joseph, MI 49085
ADMISSION: Free. Donations accepted.
ACCESSIBILITY: Fully accessible.
DESCRIPTION: The Heritage Museum and Cultural Center houses the area's history, artifacts, archival collections, and a research library in a historic building along Main Street. Carefully preserved and beautifully appointed, it presents the area's stories in spacious exhibit halls and creates new memories in elegant banquet facilities.
URL: *www.theheritagemcc.org*
CONTACT: info@theheritagemcc.org • (269) 983-1191

STURGIS

Sturgis Historical Museum

ADDRESS: 101 S. Jefferson St., Sturgis, MI 49091
ADMISSION: Free. Donations accepted.
ACCESSIBILITY: Fully accessible.
DESCRIPTION: Housed in an 1895 Tudor Revival railway depot, the museum features artifacts and exhibits on Southwest Michigan's Native American Heritage, the 11th Michigan Volunteer Infantry Regiment of the Civil War, Sturgis' town origins, The Electric City Theater, and much more. Don't forget to look up! An elevated track carries a model train throughout the museum every four minutes.

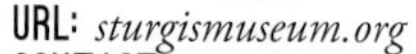

URL: *sturgismuseum.org*
CONTACT: sturgismuseum@gmail.com • (269) 503-7440

THREE OAKS

Region of Three Oaks Museum

ADDRESS: 5 Featherbone Ave., Three Oaks, MI 49128
ADMISSION: Free. Donations accepted.
ACCESSIBILITY: Contact site.
DESCRIPTION: The Region of Three Oaks Museum focuses on the history of the Three Oaks area from the days of the Potawatomi to the arrival of European settlers and beyond—including agriculture and tourism in Michiana. Current exhibits focus on early planes, trains, and automobiles; radios through the decades; and the palatial Golfmore Hotel of Grand Beach.
URL: *www.regionofthreeoaksmuseum.com*
CONTACT: trotommuseum@gmail.com • (269) 336-9688

THREE RIVERS

Sue Silliman House & Blacksmith Shop

ADDRESS: 116 S. Main St., Three Rivers, MI 49093
ADMISSION: Free. Donations accepted.
ACCESSIBILITY: Contact site.
DESCRIPTION: The Abiel Fellows Chapter of the Daughters of the American Revolution is housed in the 1876 Sue Silliman House & Blacksmith Shop. Three forges once operated in the lower level, which were reconstructed and are now used for demonstrations. A gallery upstairs showcases area history, including the Sheffield Car Company, Kellogg Farms, Tannery and Three Rivers Furs, and more.
URL: *www.dar.org/national-society/historic-sites-and-properties/sue-silliman-house-museum*
CONTACT: rjduddshank@gmail.com • (269) 435-4795

VANDALIA

Bonine House and Carriage House

ADDRESS: 18970 M-60, Vandalia, MI 49095
ADMISSION: Free. Donations accepted.
ACCESSIBILITY: Contact site.
DESCRIPTION: Quaker abolitionist James E. Bonine built this home around 1845 as a classic Greek-Revival farmhouse. It was remodeled in the Second-Empire style after the Civil War. The carriage house across the street sheltered freedom seekers on their journeys to Canada—making James E. and Sarah Bogue Bonine stationmasters on the Underground Railroad.
URL: *www.urscc.org*
CONTACT: info@urscc.org • (269) 646-0401

VICKSBURG

Vicksburg Historic Village

ADDRESS: 300 N Richardson St., Vicksburg, MI 49097
ADMISSION: Free. Donations accepted.
ACCESSIBILITY: Fully accessible.
DESCRIPTION: The Vicksburg Historic Village will transport you back in time to the turn of the century before electrification was fully realized in Vicksburg. The village includes historic Union Depot, a caboose and boxcar, print shop, village garage, Strong School, farmstead, township hall, general store, and Doris-Lee's sweet shop.

URL: *vicksburghistory.org*
CONTACT: info@vicksburghistory.org • (269) 649-1733

WEST OLIVE

Ottawa Station School House

ADDRESS: 11611 Stanton St., West Olive, MI 49460
ADMISSION: Contact site.
ACCESSIBILITY: Contact site.
DESCRIPTION: Nestled in a grouping of trees within a very quiet community, the 100-year-old former K-8 grade schoolhouse still honors the many local residents who once attended the school until it closed in 1959. Many former students still live in the area.

URL: *www.olivetownship.org/oths*
CONTACT: kitkarsten@hotmail.com • (616) 399-6939

WHITE PIGEON

U.S. Land Office Museum

ADDRESS: 113 West Chicago Rd., White Pigeon, MI 49099
ADMISSION: Contact site.
ACCESSIBILITY: Fully accessible.
DESCRIPTION: The U.S. Land Office Museum is in an original post-and-beam building housing items collected by pioneers and many original maps that share the history of White Pigeon and the surrounding area. Artifacts on display include handmade baskets, tools, clothing, and other items.

URL: *www.sjchsmi.com*
CONTACT: sjchs34@gmail.com • (269) 718-7013

Wahbememe Memorial Park

ADDRESS: 68852 U.S. 131 and intersection of U.S. 12, White Pigeon, MI 49099 White Pigeon, MI 49099
ADMISSION: Free. Donations accepted.
ACCESSIBILITY: Contact site.
DESCRIPTION: This historical site and park is home to the grave and memorial of the Potawatomi chief Wahbememe, who was known as a friend to early European-American settlers in Southern Michigan. The boulder that serves as Wahbememe's grave marker was placed by the Alba Columba Club in 1909 to honor the chief's legacy.

URL: *www.sjchsmi.com*
CONTACT: sjchs34@gmail.com • (269) 273-6003

WHITEHALL

White River Light Station and Museum

ADDRESS: 6199 Murray Rd., Whitehall, MI 49461
ADMISSION: Charge.
ACCESSIBILITY: Partially accessible.
DESCRIPTION: Built in 1875, the station guided everything from lumber schooners to resort steamships along the channel between White Lake and Lake Michigan. Visitors can learn about various lighthouse keepers, see the original fourth order Fresnel lens, climb atop the tower, or wander the beautiful grounds—which include a restored oil house and keepers' workshop.

URL: *www.splka.org*
CONTACT: splkaofficemanager@gmail.com • (231) 845-7417

ZEELAND

Dekker-Huis and Zeeland Museum

ADDRESS: 37 E. Main St., Zeeland, MI 49464
ADMISSION: Free. Donations accepted.
ACCESSIBILITY: Partially accessible.
DESCRIPTION: The museum, operated by the Zeeland Historical Society, features numerous local history displays including a pioneer room, the Zeeland State Bank, Huizenga Grocery Store, Main Street, a veteran's memorial room, and the furniture and clock-making industries. Exhibits cover Dutch immigration, the first Zeeland bank, farming, local veterans, and much more.

URL: *www.zeelandhistory.org*
CONTACT: info@zeelandhistory.org • (616) 772-4079

New Groningen Schoolhouse

ADDRESS: 10537 Paw Paw Dr., Zeeland, MI 49464
ADMISSION: Free. Donations accepted.
ACCESSIBILITY: Fully accessible.
DESCRIPTION: The New Groningen Schoolhouse dates to 1881, when it served as a rural school for children in the Zeeland and Holland area. The New Groningen Schoolhouse, restored and opened in 2011, includes an early 1900s classroom complete with desks, maps, schoolbooks, and a 40-seat meeting room available for rental. The site is operated by the Zeeland Historical Society.

URL: *www.zeelandhistory.org*
CONTACT: info@zeelandhistory.org • (616) 772-4079

CENTRAL

CENTRAL REGION

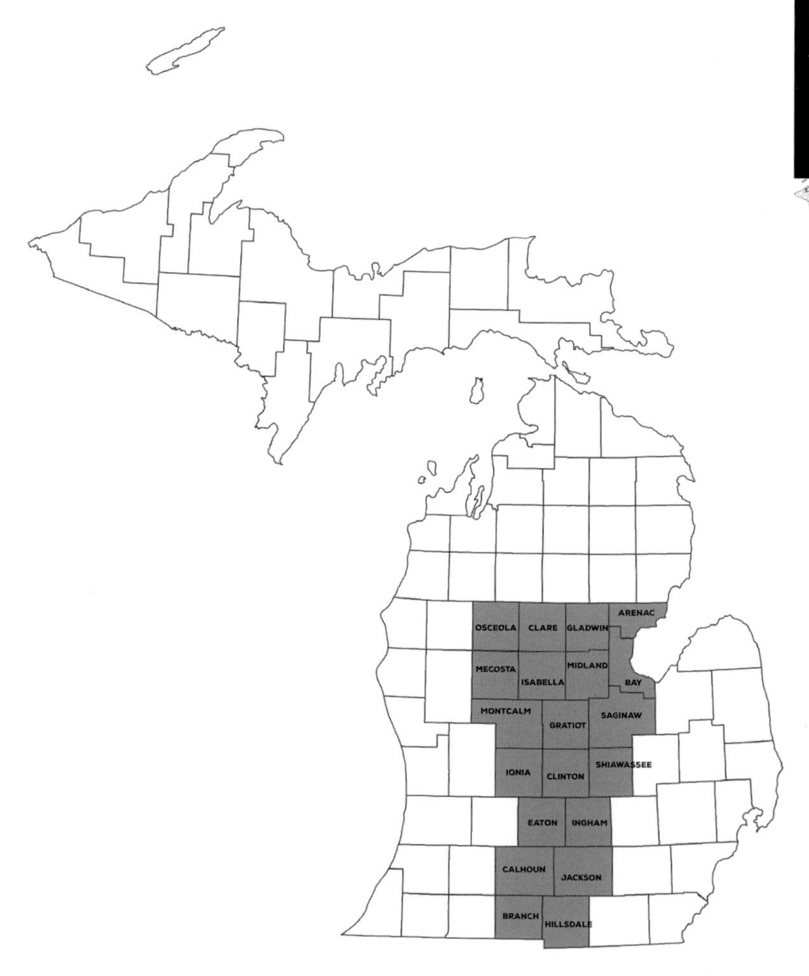

ALBION

Gardner House Museum

ADDRESS: 509 South Superior St., Albion, MI 49224
ADMISSION: Free. Donations accepted.
ACCESSIBILITY: Partially accessible.
DESCRIPTION: This Victorian house was built in 1875 by Augustus P. Gardner and displays artifacts, pictures, furniture, and many more period pieces. The first Mother's Day is believed to have originated in Albion in the late 1800s, the Purple Gang of Detroit met here in the early 1900s, and Albion is the home of three Tuskegee airmen.

URL: *www.albionhistoricalsociety.org*
CONTACT: info@albionhistoricalsociety.org • (517) 629-5100

CENTRAL

ATHENS

Athens Area Museum

ADDRESS: 101-103 S. Capital, Athens, MI 49011
ADMISSION: Free. Donations accepted.
ACCESSIBILITY: Contact site.
DESCRIPTION: In addition to offering various programs and events, the Athens Area Historical Society supports the Athens Area Museum. The society collects, preserves, and honors the heritage of the village of Athens and the surrounding area—including its past citizens, businesses, and organizations.

URL: *Facebook: Athens Area Historical Society*
CONTACT: athens.mi.historical.society@gmail.com • (269) 729-9228

BARRYTON

Barryton Area Museum

ADDRESS: 19730 30th Ave., Barryton, MI 49305
ADMISSION: Contact site.
ACCESSIBILITY: Contact site.
DESCRIPTION: The Barryton Area Historical Commission opened its museum in 1987. Visitors can enjoy exhibits showing life on the farm, home, logging, and uniforms from service personnel. There are many historical items on display including cameras, pictures, a sleigh, and artifacts from local residents. In addition to the museum, there are also one room schoolhouses to explore.

URL: *Facebook: Barryton Area Historical Museum*
CONTACT: pmcneilly7@yahoo.com • (989) 289-0238

BATH

Bath School Museum

ADDRESS: 13675 Webster Rd., Bath, MI 48808
ADMISSION: Free. Donations accepted.
ACCESSIBILITY: Fully accessible.
DESCRIPTION: Formed by citizens in 1984, the Bath School Museum showcases a unique collection of Bath School memorabilia from over 100 years, including artifacts from the Bath School Disaster of 1927. The museum is in the Bath Middle School auditorium lobby, and open during school hours and by special arrangement. Please contact us by phone prior to your visit.

URL: *www.bathschools.net/BathSchoolMuseum.aspx*
CONTACT: bath.museum1927@gmail.com • (517) 641-6721

BATTLE CREEK

Battle Creek Regional History Museum

ADDRESS: 307 W. Jackson St., Battle Creek, MI 49037
ADMISSION: Free. Donations accepted.
ACCESSIBILITY: Contact site.
DESCRIPTION: Visitors are invited to the museum to explore and learn about the history, development, and growth of the Battle Creek region. The museum is currently open as renovation and expansion occurs, so visit often to discover more about J.H. and W.K. Kellogg, Sojourner Truth, the Underground Railroad, and businesses that made their home in Battle Creek over time.
URL: *www.bcrhm.org*
CONTACT: contact@bcrhm.org • (269) 964-0750

Kimball House Museum

ADDRESS: 196 Capital Ave. NE, Battle Creek, MI 49017
ADMISSION: Charge.
ACCESSIBILITY: Partially accessible.
DESCRIPTION: The Kimball House Museum is an 1886 home previously occupied by three generations of Kimball physicians. In addition to offering a glimpse into daily family life during the Victorian era, the museum houses a major collection of artifacts and archival material relating to abolitionist and activist Sojourner Truth, who lived in Battle Creek from 1857 until her death in 1883.
URL: *www.hsbcmi.org*
CONTACT: treasurer@hsbcmi.org • (269) 660-9072

BAY CITY

Saginaw Valley Naval Ship Museum/USS Edson DD-946

ADDRESS: 1680 Martin St., Bay City, MI 48706
ADMISSION: Charge.
ACCESSIBILITY: Contact site.
DESCRIPTION: Visitors to the USS *Edson* can explore the command and control centers, berthing areas, weapons systems, and hurricane bow of the ship. On-board exhibits show how the men of the Navy lived during the Vietnam War Era. The museum also houses a flag that flew on the USS *Selfridge* on the seventh of December 1941, when Japan attacked Pearl Harbor.
URL: *www.ussedson.org*
CONTACT: info@ussedson.org • (989) 684-3946

Antique Toy and Firehouse Museum

ADDRESS: 3456 Patterson Rd., Bay City, MI 48706
ADMISSION: Charge.
ACCESSIBILITY: Contact site.
DESCRIPTION: Home to more than 60 motorized fire trucks, the Antique Toy and Firehouse Museum boasts the largest collection of fire trucks in the world, including the FDNY Super Pumper. The museum also contains more than 12,000 antique and collectible toys—many of them fire, police, and rescue vehicles.
URL: *www.toyandfirehousemuseum.org*
CONTACT: info@toyandfirehousemuseum.org • (888) 888-1270

CENTRAL

BELDING

Belding Museum

ADDRESS: 108 Hanover St., Belding, MI 48809
ADMISSION: Free. Donations accepted.
ACCESSIBILITY: Fully accessible.
DESCRIPTION: The Belding Museum occupies three floors of the historic Belrockton Dormitory. The Belrockton Dormitory was built in 1906 to house single women employed at the silk mills. The museum focuses on the silk mill industry period, which was from 1880 to 1935, as well as the history of Belding and the surrounding area.
URL: *www.ci.belding.mi.us/museum_history.php*
CONTACT: beldingmuseum@gmail.com • (616) 690-7366

BELLEVUE

Bellevue Museum

ADDRESS: 212 North Main St., Bellevue, MI 49021
ADMISSION: Contact site.
ACCESSIBILITY: Fully accessible.
DESCRIPTION: The Bellevue Museum houses local artifacts focusing on agricultural, domestic, and industrial history. Collections of the museum include genealogy and school records, period clothing, scrapbooks, and microfilm of the *Bellevue Gazette*.
URL: *www.rootsweb.com/~mibhs*
CONTACT: bellevuemihistoricalsociety@gmail.com • (269) 763-9136

BIG RAPIDS

Mecosta County Historical Society & Museum

ADDRESS: 129 S Stewart Ave., Big Rapids, MI 49307
ADMISSION: Contact site.
ACCESSIBILITY: Partially accessible.
DESCRIPTION: The society operates a museum in the former home of lumberman Fitch Phelps. The museum features exhibits that highlight Mecosta County and lumber industry history. There is a display of Native-American culture and a display on Anna Howard Shaw who grew up in Mecosta County. The museum also holds local history research collections.
URL: *www.mecostacountymuseum.com*
CONTACT: mecostacountymuseum@gmail.com • (231) 592-5091

BRECKENRIDGE

Drake Memorial House

ADDRESS: 328 E. Saginaw St., Breckenridge, MI 48615
ADMISSION: Contact site.
ACCESSIBILITY: Partially accessible.
DESCRIPTION: This is a period house set up as a 1920s doctor's office. Most items are authentic to the home and reflect the nearly 60-year medical career of Dr. Wilkie Drake, who started his career in Detroit and then moved to Breckenridge.
URL: *Facebook: Breckenridge/Wheeler Area Historical Society*
CONTACT: breckenridgewheeler@frontier.com • (989) 842-1241

Plank Road Museum

ADDRESS: 404 E. Saginaw St., Breckenridge, MI 48615
ADMISSION: Contact site.
ACCESSIBILITY: Fully accessible.
DESCRIPTION: The Plank Road Museum, operated by the Breckenridge Wheeler Area Historical Society, educates visitors on the history of the Breckenridge Area through artifacts and exhibits on farming, businesses, military, music, cultures, and schools. In addition, the research library allows guests to access a wealth of historical news accounts and oral histories.
URL: *Facebook: Breckenridge/Wheeler Area Historical Society*
CONTACT: breckenridgewheeler@frontier.com • (989) 842-1241

BRIDGEPORT

William W. Schomaker Museum

ADDRESS: 6190 Dixie Hwy., Bridgeport, MI 48722
ADMISSION: Free. Donations accepted.
ACCESSIBILITY: Fully accessible.
DESCRIPTION: The William W. Schomaker Museum houses a 1912 Model T car in perfect condition, many displays of farming and other items from early Bridgeport, an old windmill and corn crib, and even a replica outhouse. The Donna Lamb Gazebo and children's garden area surround the buildings and walkways, and nearby stands the historic 1906 Iron Bridge over the Cass River.
URL: *www.bridgeporthistorical.blogspot.com*
CONTACT: historicalsocietyofbridgeportm@gmail.com • (989) 777-5230

BROOKLYN

Cambridge Junction Historic State Park

ADDRESS: 13220 M-50, Brooklyn, MI 49230
ADMISSION: Recreation Passport required.
ACCESSIBILITY: Partially accessible.
DESCRIPTION: In the 1840s, Sylvester Walker's farmhouse tavern at Cambridge Junction was a favorite rest stop for travelers heading west on the Old Chicago Road. Visitors can tour the site's three historic buildings, view exhibits about tourism, and enjoy the natural landscape of the Irish Hills. The site is part of the Michigan History Center's Museum System.
URL: *www.michigan.gov/mhc/museums/cj*
CONTACT: mhcinfo@michigan.gov • (517) 930-3806

CHARLOTTE

1845 Eaton County Courthouse

ADDRESS: 1305 S. Cochran Ave., Charlotte, MI 48813
ADMISSION: Contact site.
ACCESSIBILITY: Contact site.
DESCRIPTION: The building served as Eaton County's courthouse from 1846 to 1872. The Greek Revival structure cost $1,000 to build in 1845. The Episcopal Church bought the courthouse in 1872. The building has served many purposes but has been renovated to resemble its original form.
URL: *www.csamuseum.net*
CONTACT: csamuseum@yahoo.com • (517) 543-6999

Courthouse Square Museum

ADDRESS: 100 W. Lawrence Ave., Charlotte, MI 48813
ADMISSION: Contact site.
ACCESSIBILITY: Partially accessible.
DESCRIPTION: The restored 1885 courthouse features ten exhibit rooms ranging from the restored courtroom to military exhibits. The building is now fully restored and serves as both a museum and wedding/event venue. Along with the courthouse, the site includes the 1873 Sheriff's residence that is currently home to the Charlotte Chamber of Commerce.
URL: *www.csamuseum.net*
CONTACT: csamuseum@yahoo.com • (517) 543-6999

CENTRAL

CHESANING

Chesaning Area Historical Museum

ADDRESS: 602 W Broad St., Chesaning, MI 48616
ADMISSION: Contact site.
ACCESSIBILITY: Fully accessible.
DESCRIPTION: Maintained and operated by the Chesaning Area Historical Society, the Chesaning Area Historical Museum is located in a late-nineteenth-century church building. Visitors of all ages are urged to come in and learn the rich history of the area through displays and permanent exhibits focusing on local Native Americans, pioneers, businesses, industries, schools, and artifacts of significance.
URL: *www.cahs.chesaning.com*
CONTACT: cahs@chesaningmuseum.net • (989) 845-3155

CLARE

Clare County Historic Park

ADDRESS: 7050 S Eberhart Ave., Clare, MI 48617
ADMISSION: Contact site.
ACCESSIBILITY: Fully accessible.
DESCRIPTION: The Clare County Historical Society invites visitors to its historic park, which includes a working blacksmith's shop, a one-room schoolhouse, log cabin, and a museum that includes exhibits that tell the history of Clare County, including the life of John "Spikehorn"Meyers.
URL: *www.clarecountyhistory.org*
CONTACT: museum@clarecountyhistory.org • (734) 755-2638

Clare Union Railroad Depot

ADDRESS: 201 W. 4th St., Clare, MI 48617
ADMISSION: Free. Donations accepted.
ACCESSIBILITY: Fully accessible.
DESCRIPTION: The Clare Union Railroad Depot was built by the Ann Arbor and Pere Marquette Railroad companies in 1896 and operated until the 1980s. After a community-driven rehabilitation project, the depot reopened its doors in 2018. The building currently houses the Depot Railroad Museum, the Clare County Arts Council, and the Clare Area Chamber of Commerce.
URL: *Facebook: Clare Union Railroad Depot*
CONTACT: jsimmer@cityofclare.org • (989) 424-4074

COLDWATER

Tibbits Opera House

ADDRESS: 14 S. Hanchett St., Coldwater, MI 49036
ADMISSION: Charge.
ACCESSIBILITY: Fully accessible.
DESCRIPTION: Built in 1882, with a beautifully restored exterior, Tibbits operates year-round with quality performances including professional summer stock, concerts, children's programming, art exhibits, community theatre, and local events. Among Michigan's oldest theatres, Tibbits is rich in history and ambiance and offers excellent acoustics in an intimate 500-seat setting.
URL: *www.tibbits.org*
CONTACT: info@tibbits.org • (517) 278-6029

CONCORD

Mann House

ADDRESS: 205 Hanover St., Concord, MI 49237
ADMISSION: Recreation Passport required.
ACCESSIBILITY: Partially accessible.
DESCRIPTION: The Mann sisters became trailblazing women dedicated to effective positive change in their community. They donated their furnished home to the Michigan Historical Commission. Visitors today can experience the family life and Victorian culture that shaped this pair of independent women. The site is part of the Michigan History Center's Museum System.
URL: *www.michigan.gov/mannhouse*
CONTACT: mhcinfo@michigan.gov • (517) 930-3806

CRYSTAL

Crystal Township Historical Society Museum

ADDRESS: 221 West Lake St., Crystal, MI 48818
ADMISSION: Free. Donations accepted.
ACCESSIBILITY: Fully accessible.
DESCRIPTION: The Crystal Township Historical Society's building houses genealogical research information for the area. There are also displays that share the history of Crystal Township and the surrounding area. The museum is open most Saturdays but can also be opened by appointment. Visitors have access to computers for research.
URL: *Facebook: Crystal Township Historical Society*
CONTACT: CTHS@CrystalHistory.com • (517) 410-7721

DURAND

Michigan Railroad History Museum

ADDRESS: 200 S. Railroad St., Durand, MI 48429
ADMISSION: Contact site.
ACCESSIBILITY: Fully accessible.
DESCRIPTION: The museum collects, preserves, and interprets artifacts, records, and documents related to the history of railroads and railroading in Michigan. It engages in activities that encourage interest in the railroad industry and is a source of information on railroad groups and structures throughout Michigan. The collection includes a wide variety of print, graphic, and railroading resources.
URL: *www.durandstation.org*
CONTACT: dusi@durandstation.org • (989) 288-3561

National Railroad Memorial

ADDRESS: Diamond District Park, Durand, MI 48429
ADMISSION: Free. Donations accepted.
ACCESSIBILITY: Contact site.
DESCRIPTION: Located in Diamond District Park, the National Railroad Memorial honors the men and women of the railroad industry and educates the public about their contributions to the history and future of Michigan and our nation. It includes monuments to those who dedicated their working life to the railroad industry and to those who made the ultimate sacrifice.
URL: *www.railroadmemorial.org*
CONTACT: info@railroadmemorial.org • (989) 249-3603

CENTRAL

EAST LANSING

Michigan State University Museum

ADDRESS: 409 West Circle Dr., East Lansing, MI 48824
ADMISSION: Free. Donations accepted.
ACCESSIBILITY: Fully accessible.
DESCRIPTION: The MSU Museum is an innovative and experimental collaboratory that exists to catalyze creativity. It is a space where people can openly explore, express, and experiment with ideas across disciplines and interests and indulge their natural curiosity about the world. It is accredited by the American Alliance of Museums and is the state's first Smithsonian Affiliate.
URL: *www.museum.msu.edu*
CONTACT: palagyis@msu.edu • (517) 884-6897

Michigan State University Archives & Historical Collections

ADDRESS: 943 Conrad Rd., Conrad Hall, Room 101 East Lansing, MI 48824
ADMISSION: Contact site.
ACCESSIBILITY: Fully accessible.
DESCRIPTION: The MSU Archives shares 160 years of Spartan history including photographs, films, letters, diaries, scrapbooks, and maps. The University Archives is open to the general public and is a great resource for researchers, students of all ages, local history enthusiasts, and genealogists. Changing exhibits are available to the public.
URL: *www.archives.msu.edu*
CONTACT: archives@msu.edu • (517) 355-2330

EATON RAPIDS

G.A.R. Memorial Hall & Museum

ADDRESS: 224 South Main St., Eaton Rapids, MI 48827
ADMISSION: Free. Donations accepted.
ACCESSIBILITY: Fully accessible.
DESCRIPTION: The G.A.R. Memorial Hall & Museum is dedicated to the Grand Army of the Republic (G.A.R.), an organization created by the Union veterans of the Civil War. The museum is in the actual 1886 G.A.R. Post building that the veterans used and just a block away from G.A.R. Island Park, where Civil War veterans held annual reunions for many years.
URL: *www.garmuseum.com*
CONTACT: garmichigan@gmail.com • (517) 992-6427

EDMORE

Old Fence Rider Historical Center Museum

ADDRESS: 222 Sheldon St., Edmore, MI 48829
ADMISSION: Free. Donations accepted.
ACCESSIBILITY: Fully accessible.
DESCRIPTION: The Old Fence Rider Historical Center Museum contains displays on local history, early America, pioneers, the logging industry, the Civil War, and the major wars of the twentieth century. Also included are life-size recreations of an old-fashioned drugstore and gas station and a 1950s diner.
URL: *Facebook: Old Fence Rider Historical Center Museum*
CONTACT: cjlon49@yahoo.com • (989) 427-1032

ESSEXVILLE

Heritage House Farm Museum

ADDRESS: 305 Pine St., Essexville, MI 48732
ADMISSION: Contact site.
ACCESSIBILITY: Contact site.
DESCRIPTION: The Heritage House Farm Museum is a fully furnished nine-room home from the early 1890s. The home was built by John Garber, whose family members were the building's only residents. Today, the home features furniture that belonged to both the Garber family and the community. Also on site are a German-style shed, and corn crib.
URL: *Facebook: Heritage House*
CONTACT: lenglehardt7025@charter.net • (989) 893-6186

EVART

Evart Public Library and Museum

ADDRESS: 104 North Main St., Evart, MI 49631
ADMISSION: Free. Donations accepted.
ACCESSIBILITY: Fully accessible.
DESCRIPTION: The Evart Public Library and Museum has rotating exhibits and freestanding items relating to the history of the Evart area and its citizens. Collections include artifacts, records, and archival materials—such as cemetery records for nearby communities, microfilm of *The Evart Review*, and family histories.
URL: *www.evart.org/our_community/library_2.php*
CONTACT: evartlibrary@yahoo.com • (231) 734-5542

FARWELL

Farwell Area Historical Museum

ADDRESS: 221 West Main St., Farwell, MI 48622
ADMISSION: Contact site.
ACCESSIBILITY: Fully accessible.
DESCRIPTION: Built for the Farwell Ladies Library Association in the early 1880s, the structure now houses the Farwell Area Historical Museum. The museum offers information about the development and history of Farwell. Visitors can learn about early life in the village through historical household items, clothes, utensils, photos, and more.
URL: *www.farwellmuseum.com*
CONTACT: ajwilson12002@yahoo.com • (989) 588-9653

FRANKENMUTH

Michigan Heroes Museum

ADDRESS: 1250 Weiss St., Frankenmuth, MI 48734
ADMISSION: Charge.
ACCESSIBILITY: Fully accessible.
DESCRIPTION: The Michigan Heroes Museum is home to more than 140 displays, telling the story of more than 900 servicemen and women. Highlights of the collections include the uniforms of 5 Michigan governors and 13 Michigan astronauts. The museum also features the stories of 30 individual Medal of Honor recipients.
URL: *www.miheroes.org*
CONTACT: info@miheroes.org • (989) 652-8005

GRAND LEDGE

Grand Ledge Area Historical Society Museum

ADDRESS: 118 West Lincoln St., Grand Ledge, MI 48837
ADMISSION: Free. Donations accepted.
ACCESSIBILITY: Fully accessible.
DESCRIPTION: The Grand Ledge Area Historical Society Museum is housed in an 1880 Gothic Revival house and exhibits explore a new theme each year. Archives and photographs are housed at the Grand Ledge District Library. The collection includes local photographs and slides, archival materials on businesses, cultural activities, families, schools, churches, and genealogical research materials.
URL: *www.glhistoricalsociety.org*
CONTACT: glhistory1975@gmail.com • (517) 627-3149

GRASS LAKE

Dewey School Museum

ADDRESS: 11501 Territorial Rd., Grass Lake, MI 48340
ADMISSION: Charge.
ACCESSIBILITY: Contact site.
DESCRIPTION: The Dewey School Museum conducts school tours in an effort to help students experience and appreciate nineteenth-century rural schooling. Its parent organization, the Waterloo Area Historical Society, also hopes to foster an appreciation of the pioneer farmers of Michigan, their family life, and their children's schooling.
URL: *www.waterloofarmmuseum.org*
CONTACT: info@waterloofarmmuseum.org • (804) 596-2254

Waterloo Farm Museum

ADDRESS: 13493 Waterloo Munith Rd., Grass Lake, MI 49240
ADMISSION: Charge.
ACCESSIBILITY: Partially accessible.
DESCRIPTION: The Waterloo Farm Museum homestead includes several buildings, including an 1865 farmhouse, barns, a milk house, a log cabin, a workshop with forge, an icehouse, and a windmill. Visitors will also get the chance to explore historical artifacts from Michigan farming and country living, including farm equipment and household items.
URL: *www.waterloofarmmuseum.org*
CONTACT: info@waterloofarmmuseum.org • (804) 596-2254

Lost Railway Museum

ADDRESS: 142 W Michigan Ave., Grass Lake, MI 49240
ADMISSION: Contact site.
ACCESSIBILITY: Fully accessible.
DESCRIPTION: Learn about the interurban railway system at the Lost Railway Museum. Notable features include a video presentation of the interurban systems between 1900–1930, two authentic interurban cars under restoration, as well as multiple displays and kiosks of historical artifacts and articles related to interurban history.
URL: *www.lostrailwaymuseum.org*
CONTACT: info@lostrailwaymuseum.org • (517) 522-9500

GREENVILLE

Fighting Falcon Military Museum

ADDRESS: 516 W. Cass St., Greenville, MI 48838
ADMISSION: Free. Donations accepted.
ACCESSIBILITY: Fully accessible.
DESCRIPTION: The primary focus of the museum's exhibits center on WWII, but artifacts from the Civil War, WWI, Korean War, Vietnam, and modern conflicts are also displayed. The restoration of an Army Air Corps CG4A, known worldwide as the "Fighting Falcon," showcases an iconic piece of Greenville history. Visitors can try their hand at landing the glider in a simulation.
URL: *www.thefightingfalcon.com*
CONTACT: Contact via website. • (616) 225-1940

Flat River Historical Society and Museum

ADDRESS: 213 North Franklin St., Greenville, MI 48848
ADMISSION: Contact site.
ACCESSIBILITY: Partially accessible.
DESCRIPTION: The "Main Street Greenville" period rooms let visitors feel they are walking through history as they view the shops and homes that may have been here in the past. Other exhibits feature refrigerator companies as well as items from the lumbering and farming prevalent in the area long ago. A Victorian Garden next to the building is a favorite for family and special occasion photos.
URL: *www.flatrivermuseum.org*
CONTACT: frhsmuseum@gmail.com • (616) 754-5296

Oakfield Museum

ADDRESS: 11009 Podunk Ave. NE, Greenville, MI 48838
ADMISSION: Free. Donations accepted.
ACCESSIBILITY: Partially accessible.
DESCRIPTION: The building that houses the museum was built as the meeting hall of the Ancient Order of Gleaners, an insurance company for agricultural workers. Displays include Gleaner memorabilia and community artifacts. Other items include a rural postal carrier sleigh and a Stevens dishwasher patented in 1886.
URL: *www.commoncorners.com/kent/kent_oakfield_museum.htm*
CONTACT: oakfieldmuseum@gmail.com • (616) 485-3404

HANOVER

Conklin Reed Organ and History Museum

ADDRESS: 105 Fairview St., Hanover, MI 49241
ADMISSION: Charge.
ACCESSIBILITY: Partially accessible.
DESCRIPTION: The Conklin Reed Organ and History Museum began with the 73 organs of Mr. Lee Conklin's original collection and has since grown into one of the largest public collections of playable antique pump organs in the world. The museum also features several displays on local and general history, as well as volunteer-led organ restoration workshops.
URL: *www.hhahs.org*
CONTACT: hhahsmichigan@gmail.com • (517) 563-8927

Hanover-Horton Heritage Park

ADDRESS: 121 Tefft St., Hanover, MI 49241
ADMISSION: Free. Donations accepted.
ACCESSIBILITY: Partially accessible.
DESCRIPTION: The Hanover-Horton Area Historical Society's Heritage Park showcases local agricultural history with its vintage working sawmill and planer, maple sugar shack, antique farm equipment barn, historical log cabin, small wooden barn, event center, nature trails, and flower gardens. The property is open year-round for hiking, horseback riding, special events, and more.
URL: *www.hhahs.org*
CONTACT: hhahsmichigan@gmail.com • (517) 563-8927

HARRISON TOWNSHIP

Selfridge Military Air Museum

ADDRESS: 27333 C St., Bldg. 1011, Selfridge ANG Base, Harrison Township, MI 48045
ADMISSION: Charge.
ACCESSIBILITY: Fully accessible.
DESCRIPTION: The museum includes items for all past and present military units at Selfridge Air National Guard Base in the Michigan Air National Guard. Museum buildings have displays of military artifacts including photographs, uniforms, engines, and items of interest. On display are more than 30 aircraft, vehicles, and missiles.
URL: *www.selfridgeairmuseum.org*
CONTACT: info@selfridgeairmuseum.org • (586) 239-5035

HILLSDALE

Will Carleton Poorhouse

ADDRESS: 180 N. Wolcott Dr., Hillsdale, MI 49242
ADMISSION: Free. Donations accepted.
ACCESSIBILITY: Contact site.
DESCRIPTION: Experience yesteryear at the Will Carleton Poorhouse, which is open for special events and for arranged tours. The museum features many restored artifacts and plays host to several changing exhibits that highlight the history of the poorhouse and the surrounding area.
URL: *www.hillsdalehistoricalsociety.org*
CONTACT: hillsdalehistoricalsociety@gmail.com • (517) 212-0776

HOMER

Blair Historical Farm

ADDRESS: 26445 M-60, East Homer, MI 49245
ADMISSION: Contact site.
ACCESSIBILITY: Partially accessible.
DESCRIPTION: The Blair Historical Farm is run by the Homer Historical Society and has an 1870s home on its grounds to share how people lived in the late 1800s. Also on the grounds are an 1920s barn, a more modern barn that houses a Birdsell Clover Huller, the 1889 Albion Township Town Hall, a DT&M way station, and a carriage house.
URL: *www.homerhistoricalsociety.org*
CONTACT: Contact via website. • (517) 568-3920

IONIA

Blanchard House & Museum

ADDRESS: 251 East Main St., Ionia, MI 48846
ADMISSION: Free. Donations accepted.
ACCESSIBILITY: Contact site.
DESCRIPTION: The Blanchard House showcases what upper-class life was like in the late 1800s, while also sharing the history of Ionia and the heritage of the people who lived here before it was called "Ionia." The basement level of the Blanchard House serves as a local history museum, highlighting the documents and artifacts collected by the Ionia County Historical Society.
URL: *www.ioniahistory.org*
CONTACT: info@ioniahistory.org • (616) 527-6281

ITHACA

Gratiot County Area Historical Museum

ADDRESS: 129 West Center St., Ithaca, MI 48847
ADMISSION: Contact site.
ACCESSIBILITY: Fully accessible.
DESCRIPTION: The Gratiot County Area Historical Museum is housed in a Victorian house built in 1881, which is on the State Register of Historic Sites. Collections include furniture, ceramics, glass, china, kitchenware, clothing, needlework, photographs, and postcards from the 1850s to the 1950s. A barn with small farm implements and tools is also featured.
URL: *www.gchgs.org*
CONTACT: info@gchgs.org • (989) 875-6232

JONESVILLE

Grosvenor House Museum

ADDRESS: 211 Maumee St., Jonesville, MI 49250
ADMISSION: Contact site.
ACCESSIBILITY: Contact site.
DESCRIPTION: Visit the renovated 32-room home of E.O. Grosvenor, one-time Lt. Governor of Michigan. Mr. Grosvenor was head of the commission in charge of building the Michigan state capitol building, and his home was designed by the same architect as the capitol.
URL: *grosvenorhouse.wordpress.com*
CONTACT: grosvenorhousemuseum@outlook.com • (517) 849-9596

LAKEVIEW

Lakeview Area Museum

ADDRESS: 107 N. Lincoln St., Lakeview, MI 48850
ADMISSION: Contact site.
ACCESSIBILITY: Contact site.
DESCRIPTION: The museum contains an array of artifacts from the lumbering industry, businesses, clubs, organizations, schooling, and citizens of the town's past. Outside the museum stands the historic jail house and an old horse-drawn snowplow. If you enjoy learning about small town history or are curious about the history of the area, the Lakeview Area Museum provides many resources.
URL: *Facebook: Lakeview Area Museum*
CONTACT: lakeviewareamuseum@gmail.com • (989) 352-7304

LANSING

Michigan History Museum

ADDRESS: 702 W. Kalamazoo St., Lansing, MI 48909
ADMISSION: Charge.
ACCESSIBILITY: Fully accessible.
DESCRIPTION: The Michigan History Museum is a family-friendly place where people of all ages can have fun actively learning about their heritage and the history of Michigan through exhibits, special events, and diverse programming. Immersive displays and hands-on activities bring Michigan history to life—from the ice age through to the late twentieth century.
URL: *www.michigan.gov/mhc*
CONTACT: mhcinfo@michigan.gov • (517) 335-2573

Library of Michigan

ADDRESS: 702 W. Kalamazoo St., Lansing, MI 48915
ADMISSION: Free. Donations accepted.
ACCESSIBILITY: Fully accessible.
DESCRIPTION: Since 1828, the Library of Michigan has served Michigan by collecting, preserving, and providing access to the story of the State. Come visit your premier resource for Michigan's history and literature and uncover details of your community through the library's extensive collection of Michigan newspapers, maps, published histories, rare items, and more.
URL: *www.michigan.gov/libraryofmichigan*
CONTACT: librarian@michigan.gov • (517) 335-1477

Michigan State Capitol

ADDRESS: 100 North Capitol Ave., Lansing, MI 48933
ADMISSION: Free. Donations accepted.
ACCESSIBILITY: Fully accessible.
DESCRIPTION: The Michigan State Capitol, a symbol of the rise and progress of Michigan, opened in 1879 to great acclaim. Along with tours, visitors can view parts of the Battle Flags collection and informational panels and historical artifacts in the new Heritage Hall. The capitol was designated a National Historic Landmark in 1992.
URL: *www.capitol.michigan.gov*
CONTACT: (517) 373-2353

R.E. Olds Transportation Museum

ADDRESS: 240 Museum Dr., Lansing, MI 48933
ADMISSION: Charge.
ACCESSIBILITY: Fully accessible.
DESCRIPTION: Experience a slice of Lansing's history through the lens of transportation. View vehicles that were built in Lansing from some of the earliest models to the latest, as well as photographs, artifacts, and documents. This industrial museum in the capital city is sure to impress.

URL: *www.reoldsmuseum.org*
CONTACT: autos@reoldsmuseum.org • (517) 372-0529

Turner-Dodge House

ADDRESS: 100 E. North St., Lansing, MI 48906
ADMISSION: Contact site.
ACCESSIBILITY: Partially accessible.
DESCRIPTION: The historic Turner-Dodge House was built in 1858 by Marion and James Turner and enlarged in 1903 by daughter Abby and her husband, Frank Dodge. Guests learn the history of the Turner and Dodge families and enjoy historical exhibits throughout the home. Guided tours are available, and the house may also be rented for special events.

URL: *www.lansingmi.gov/938/Turner-Dodge-House*
CONTACT: barbara.loyer@lansingmi.gov • (517) 483-4220

LESLIE

Leslie Area Historical Society & Museum

ADDRESS: 107 E. Bellevue St., Leslie, MI 49251
ADMISSION: Free. Donations accepted.
ACCESSIBILITY: Contact site.
DESCRIPTION: The Leslie Area Historical Society & Museum is in G.A.R. Hall, which was originally built in 1903 as a meeting place for Civil War veterans. On display are records and artifacts. Notable exhibits feature *Paddle-to-the-Sea* author Holling C. Holling and Chef Frank White, whose likeness appeared on Cream of Wheat from 1901–2020.

URL: *www.lesliehistorical.org*
CONTACT: info@lesliehistorical.org • (517) 712-5459

MARSHALL

Governor's Mansion Museum

ADDRESS: 612 S Marshall Ave., Marshall, MI 49068
ADMISSION: Charge.
ACCESSIBILITY: Contact site.
DESCRIPTION: The Governor's Mansion Museum is located within the 1839 home of Michigan's third governor, James Wright Gordon. The beautiful Greek Revival home is filled with antiques from the 1800s that tell state and local history, including the story of the Crosswhite Case.

URL: *Facebook: Marshalls Governors Mansion*
CONTACT: marshallmuseum@gmail.com • (269) 781-5260

Honolulu House Museum

ADDRESS: 107 N. Kalamazoo Ave., Marshall, MI 49068
ADMISSION: Charge.
ACCESSIBILITY: Partially accessible.
DESCRIPTION: The Honolulu House was built in 1860 by Abner Pratt, then-consul to the Sandwich Islands. The exterior architecture is a blend of Italianate, Gothic, and Polynesian. The interior features paint-on-plaster wall and ceiling paintings restored to the splendor of the 1880s, including period furnishings and authentic replicas of the carpets.
URL: *www.marshallhistoricalsociety.com*
CONTACT: info@marshallhistoricalsociety.org • (269) 781-8544

CENTRAL

Marshall Historical Museum at the G.A.R. Hall

ADDRESS: 402 E. Michigan Ave., Marshall, MI 49068
ADMISSION: Charge.
ACCESSIBILITY: Partially accessible.
DESCRIPTION: This museum focuses on telling Marshall's stories and highlighting items made in the town. Some items of interest are a Marshall folding bathtub, a buggy made by Page Brothers Buggy Works, and items from the Brewer Dry Goods Store. The building containing the museum's collections was built in 1902 as a meeting place for Civil War veterans.
URL: *www.marshallhistoricalsociety.com*
CONTACT: info@marshallhistoricalsociety.org • (269) 781-8544

Capitol Hill School

ADDRESS: 602 E. Washington St., Marshall, MI 49068
ADMISSION: Charge.
ACCESSIBILITY: Partially accessible.
DESCRIPTION: Built in 1860 near the site intended to be the Michigan State Capitol, Capitol Hill School is the only survivor of three identical Gothic Revival schools. It was removed from public service in 1961 but continues to provide a turn-of-the-century classroom experience. The building is listed on the National Register of Historic Places and the Historic American Buildings Survey.
URL: *www.marshallhistoricalsociety.com*
CONTACT: info@marshallhistoricalsociety.org • (269) 781-8544

Marshall Postal Museum

ADDRESS: 202 E Michigan Ave., Marshall, MI 49068
ADMISSION: Charge.
ACCESSIBILITY: Contact site.
DESCRIPTION: The Marshall Postal Museum is the second-largest postal museum in the nation. Located in the basement of the Marshall Post Office and open by appointment only, the guided tour takes around one hour. On display are a 1931 Model A mail truck, three different mail buggies, store front post offices, and hundreds of other postal items.
URL: *www.marshallmich.net/post_office_museum*
CONTACT: mikeschragg@gmail.com • (269) 781-2859

MASON

Mason Historical Museum

ADDRESS: 200 East Oak St., Mason, MI 48854
ADMISSION: Contact site.
ACCESSIBILITY: Fully accessible.
DESCRIPTION: The Mason Historical Museum contains several themed rooms showcasing artifacts related to the history of the Mason area. In the library, visitors will find photos, books, files, and DVDs pertaining to past programs. The Mason Historical Society, which manages the museum, also provides historical lectures, presentations, and family events for the public.
URL: *www.masonmuseum.com*
CONTACT: masonmuseum1865@gmail.com • (517) 676-5974

Pink School

ADDRESS: 707 W. Ash St., Mason, MI 48854
ADMISSION: Contact site.
ACCESSIBILITY: Fully accessible.
DESCRIPTION: The Pink School is a one-room school that originally opened in 1854. It displays old school memorabilia, including the original slate blackboard and rope to pull the bell. The school was open for 111 years, and there is a photo for each of the 105 teachers who worked at the school.

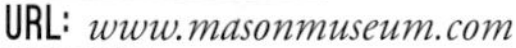

URL: *www.masonmuseum.com*
CONTACT: masonmuseum1865@gmail.com • (517) 676-5974

MIDLAND

Alden B. Dow Home & Studio

ADDRESS: 315 Post St., Midland, MI 48640
ADMISSION: Contact site.
ACCESSIBILITY: Contact site.
DESCRIPTION: The Alden B. Dow Home & Studio was the home of Alden B. Dow, an organic architect. Today, his home, along with his studio, is a National Historic Landmark that is open for tours and educational programming. On display are original furnishings, a 1930s–1960s ceramic and glass collection, personal and professional libraries, historical model-scale trains, and mechanical toys.
URL: *www.abdow.org*
CONTACT: info@abdow.org • (989) 839-2744

Chippewa Nature Center

ADDRESS: 400 South Badour Rd., Midland, MI 48640
ADMISSION: Free. Donations accepted.
ACCESSIBILITY: Fully accessible.
DESCRIPTION: The Chippewa Nature Center seeks to connect all people with nature through educational, recreational, and cultural experiences by way of its visitor center; 19 miles of trails; and its 1870s homestead consisting of a cabin, one-room schoolhouse, timber-frame barn, sugarhouse, heirloom garden, and more. At the latter, visitors can enjoy farm animals and historical programs.
URL: *www.chippewanaturecenter.org*
CONTACT: info@chippewanaturecenter.org • (989) 631-0830

CENTRAL

Doan Midland County History Center

ADDRESS: 3417 West Main St., Midland, MI 48640
ADMISSION: Contact site.
ACCESSIBILITY: Fully accessible.
DESCRIPTION: The Herbert D. Doan Midland County History Center is the gateway to Heritage Park. It houses a permanent hands-on gallery of interactive exhibits of Midland County history, from the beginning to today. Among the many features of the center are a gallery of featured exhibitions, a research library for local and general history, and an archival collection of Midland County artifacts.
URL: *www.midlandcenter.org*
CONTACT: info@midlandcenter.org • (989) 631-8250

Dow Gardens

ADDRESS: 1018 W. Main St., Midland, MI 48640
ADMISSION: Charge.
ACCESSIBILITY: Fully accessible.
DESCRIPTION: Established as the home of Herbert H. and Grace A. Dow in 1899, today Dow Gardens offers 110 acres of award-winning horticulture, dynamic programming, and a canopy walk. History lovers will enjoy adding a ticket to tour The Pines, the former home of Herbert H. and Grace A. Dow, to their admission purchase.
URL: *www.dowgardens.org*
CONTACT: info@dowgardens.org • (800) 362-4874

Heritage Park

ADDRESS: 3417 West Main St., Midland, MI 48640
ADMISSION: Contact site.
ACCESSIBILITY: Partially accessible.
DESCRIPTION: Heritage Park is home to multiple historical sites. The 1874 Bradley Home is a historic house museum. The adjacent Carriage House hosts a collection of horse-drawn carriages and sleighs and is home to mid-Michigan's largest functioning blacksmith's shop. View the multimedia exhibits in the Herbert H. Dow Historical Museum to learn about Midland's largest business.
URL: *www.midlandcenter.org*
CONTACT: info@midlandcenter.org • (989) 631-8250

MOUNT PLEASANT

Museum of Cultural and Natural History

ADDRESS: 650 E. Bellows, CMU Campus Rowe Hall 103, Mount Pleasant, MI 48859
ADMISSION: Free. Donations accepted.
ACCESSIBILITY: Fully accessible.
DESCRIPTION: Permanent exhibits include mastodons and natural history scenes. Collections focus on history, anthropology, zoology, and geology of the Great Lakes region. The museum also includes the collection of the Isabella County Historical Society.
URL: *www.museum.cmich.edu*
CONTACT: cmuseum@cmich.edu • (989) 774-3829

Bohannon Schoolhouse / Gerald L. Poor Museum

ADDRESS: 1303 West Campus Dr., Mount Pleasant, MI 48859
ADMISSION: Free. Donations accepted.
ACCESSIBILITY: Fully accessible.
DESCRIPTION: The Poor Museum inside the 1901 Bohannon Schoolhouse provides a period representation of one-room schoolhouses in Michigan, complete with exhibits that focus on the schools of Isabella County, Michigan, and the history of Central Michigan University.
URL: *www.museum.cmich.edu*
CONTACT: cmuseum@cmich.edu • (989) 774-3829

Clarke Historical Library

ADDRESS: Park Library 142B Central Michigan University, Mount Pleasant, MI 48859
ADMISSION: Free. Donations accepted.
ACCESSIBILITY: Fully accessible.
DESCRIPTION: The Clarke Historical Library has a comprehensive printed collection related to Michigan history. Its archives focus primarily on the region north of Lansing and south of Mackinac. The library also serves as the Central Michigan University archives.
URL: *www.cmich.edu/research/clarke-historical-library*
CONTACT: clarke@cmich.edu • (989) 774-3864

OKEMOS

Meridian Historical Village

ADDRESS: 5151 Marsh Rd., Okemos, MI 48864
ADMISSION: Charge.
ACCESSIBILITY: Partially accessible.
DESCRIPTION: The Meridian Historical Village is a nineteenth-century living history museum with nine historic structures, including a one-room schoolhouse, tollhouse, farmhouse, barn, general store, tavern and inn, and log cabin. It features a small archival collection of local materials. Some of the buildings, including the chapel, may be rented.
URL: *www.meridianhistoricalvillage.org*
CONTACT: meridianhistoricalvillage@gmail.com • (517) 347-7300

Nokomis Cultural Heritage Center

ADDRESS: 5153 Marsh Rd., Okemos, MI 48864
ADMISSION: Free. Donations accepted.
ACCESSIBILITY: Fully accessible.
DESCRIPTION: The center is a Native-American cultural learning center dedicated to the preservation and presentation of Anishinaabe culture. Weekly Language and Craft night programs, changing displays, and traditional celebrations engage the local native community in the continuation of Anishnaabe knowledge. The center has both a hands-on learning center and a gallery.
URL: *www.nokomis.org*
CONTACT: info@nokomis.org • (517) 349-5777

CENTRAL

OVID

Ovid Historical Society

ADDRESS: 131 East Williams, Ovid, MI 48866
ADMISSION: Contact site.
ACCESSIBILITY: Contact site.
DESCRIPTION: Return to yesteryear in the Mary Myers Museum, which is housed in an 1869 Italianate-style structure that is furnished for the period and operated by the Ovid Historical Society. Many of the items in the museum were donated by local residents wanting to share their love of history.

URL: *www.ovidhistoricalsociety.weebly.com*
CONTACT: (989) 834-5421

OWOSSO

Shiawassee County Historical Society Archives & Museum

ADDRESS: 1997 N. M52, Owosso, MI 48867
ADMISSION: Free. Donations accepted.
ACCESSIBILITY: Fully accessible.
DESCRIPTION: The Shiawassee County Historical Society collects and displays items pertaining to county history—especially those related to family histories and the county's beginnings. The society's collections include household artifacts, farm equipment, period clothing, Native tools and stones, buggies, and mammoth tusks.

URL: *www.shiawasseecountyhistsoc.org*
CONTACT: archer@charter.net • (989) 723-2371

REED CITY

Reed City Heritage Museum

ADDRESS: 138 W. Slosson Ave., Reed City, MI 49677
ADMISSION: Free. Donations accepted.
ACCESSIBILITY: Fully accessible.
DESCRIPTION: Visit our museum to see a memorial to Rev. George Bennard, author of the famous hymn "The Old Rugged Cross," as well as artifacts pertinent to the historical significance of Osceola County and surrounding communities. The collection includes early-twentieth-century items related to logging, manufacturing, oil wells, transportation, households, the military, and more.

URL: *Facebook: Reed City Heritage Museum*
CONTACT: rcheritagemuseum@gmail.com • (231) 590-5805

REMUS

Remus Area Historical Society

ADDRESS: 324 S Sheridan Ave., Remus, MI 49340
ADMISSION: Free. Donations accepted.
ACCESSIBILITY: Fully accessible.
DESCRIPTION: The society preserves the heritage of Remus and surrounding areas. We hope to generate interest, encourage historical research, and bring a better understanding of how the settlers and early residents laid the foundations for our current way of life. On display are artifacts and pictures of local families, businesses, churches, veterans, schools, and the Remus Creamery.

URL: *www.remus.org/museum-historical-society*
CONTACT: remusmuseum@gmail.com • Contact via website.

SAGINAW

Castle Museum

ADDRESS: 500 Federal Ave., Saginaw, MI 48607
ADMISSION: Charge.
ACCESSIBILITY: Fully accessible.
DESCRIPTION: Built in 1898 as a French Renaissance Revival style U.S. post office, The Castle Museum of Saginaw County History offers three floors of about 40 exhibits—temporary and permanent—including the Saginaw County Sports Hall of Fame. The Historical Society of Saginaw County maintains and preserves the collection of more than 100,000 artifacts used for exhibits and research.
URL: *www.castlemuseum.org*
CONTACT: azehnder@castlemuseum.org • (989) 752-2861

Saginaw Railway Museum

ADDRESS: 900 Maple St., Saginaw, MI 48602
ADMISSION: Free. Donations accepted.
ACCESSIBILITY: Partially accessible.
DESCRIPTION: The building that houses the Saginaw Railway Museum was built by the Pere Marquette Railway in 1907. It is located on the active Lake State Railway mainline. The Saginaw Valley Railroad Historical Society operates an HO Scale model train display in the basement, and a changing display of artifacts, tools, photos, and maps conveys railway history, lore, and legends.
URL: *Facebook: Saginaw Railway Museum*
CONTACT: info@saginawrailwaymuseum.org • (989) 792-7994

ST. CHARLES

St. Charles Area Museum

ADDRESS: 103 South Saginaw St., Saint Charles, MI 48655
ADMISSION: Free. Donations accepted.
ACCESSIBILITY: Fully accessible.
DESCRIPTION: Visit the St. Charles Area Museum located in downtown St. Charles. Visitors can enjoy seeing a restored 1941 Chessie Caboose—one of three remaining of its type—and displays on logging, coal mining, and the military.
URL: *Facebook: St. Charles Area Museum*
CONTACT: stcharlesareamuseum@gmail.com • (989) 865-9115

SANFORD

Sanford Centennial Museum

ADDRESS: 2222 Smith St., Sanford, MI 48657
ADMISSION: Free. Donations accepted.
ACCESSIBILITY: Contact site.
DESCRIPTION: In 1970, the town of Sanford celebrated its centennial and set up a commemorative historical exhibit in the empty 1910 schoolhouse. The exhibit was so successful, the town decided to make it permanent. The Sanford Historical Society was then created to manage the museum and has since moved and reconstructed eight local historic buildings in danger of being torn down.
URL: *www.sanfordhist.org*
CONTACT: logmarks@sanfordhist.org • (989) 687-9048

CENTRAL

SARANAC

Grand Trunk Saranac Depot

ADDRESS: 138 N Bridge St., Saranac, MI 48881
ADMISSION: Contact site.
ACCESSIBILITY: Fully accessible.
DESCRIPTION: The restored 1907 Grand Trunk Saranac Depot, located on the banks of the Grand River, is operated by the Boston-Saranac Historical Society. The depot's collections consist of historical artifacts donated from area families. Also on site are a 1900 Grand Trunk Caboose filled with railroad memorabilia, a 1946 John Bean Pumper fire truck, and antique sleighs and carriages.
URL: *Facebook: Boston Saranac Historical Society*
CONTACT: marilar@att.net • (616) 693-2730

SIDNEY

Montcalm Heritage Village

ADDRESS: 2800 College Dr., Sidney, MI 48885
ADMISSION: Contact site.
ACCESSIBILITY: Partially accessible.
DESCRIPTION: The village is a collection of 21 buildings, which include a schoolhouse, log cabin, hat shop, doctor's house, blacksmith shed, country store, jailhouse, and church. Visitors can tour on their own or arrange for guided tours to see the insides of the buildings and learn more about their significance. History is more than a picture at Montcalm Heritage Village!
URL: *www.montcalm.edu/heritage-village*
CONTACT: room.reservations@montcalm.edu • (989) 328-2111

ST. JOHNS

Clinton County Historical Museum

ADDRESS: 106 Maple St., St. Johns, MI 48879
ADMISSION: Free. Donations accepted.
ACCESSIBILITY: Contact site.
DESCRIPTION: Visit the oldest brick home in St. Johns to see life in the late 1800s, including the General Store and Carriage House representing life and times of years ago. St. Johns was home to a bicycle band and there is a life-size high wheel bicycle sculpture by Ivan Iler on the grounds.
URL: *www.pgsmuseum.com*
CONTACT: museum@cchistoricalmuseum.org • (989) 224-2894.

ST. LOUIS

St. Louis Area Historical Society Museum

ADDRESS: 110 Crawford St., St. Louis, MI 48880
ADMISSION: Free. Donations accepted.
ACCESSIBILITY: Fully accessible.
DESCRIPTION: With a historic park, train depot, log cabin, and transportation pavilion, the St. Louis Area Historical Society offers visitors a look into the history of the city of St. Louis and the townships of Bethany and Pine River. Signage allows visitors to take a self-conducted tour of the society's grounds.
URL: *www.stlouismi.com/1/stlouis/Historical_Society.asp*
CONTACT: st.louishistoricalsociety@gmail.com • (989) 763-2943

TEKONSHA

Tekonsha Historical Society Museum

ADDRESS: 109 East Canal St., Tekonsha, MI 49092
ADMISSION: Free. Donations accepted.
ACCESSIBILITY: Fully accessible.
DESCRIPTION: The museum has many replica hand-built homes from the town, a reference library, photos, and memorabilia. The museum is readily available to anyone wishing to trace his or her family ancestry or to learn more about the history of Tekonsha. Please contact the site to arrange for access to the museum.
URL: *No website.*
CONTACT: bc.arnold765@gmail.com • (517) 765-2588

UNION CITY

Hammond House Museum

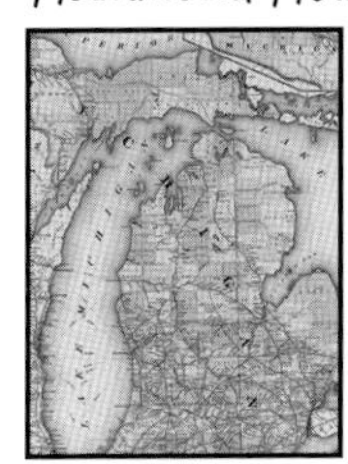

ADDRESS: 210 Charlotte St., Union City, MI 49094
ADMISSION: Contact site.
ACCESSIBILITY: Contact site.
DESCRIPTION: The 150-year-old Hammond House is a Greek Revival style structure and was one of the first fine homes in Union City. On display are historical household items and memorabilia from the surrounding area, as well as a collection of watercolors by local artist J.P. Palmer. The former Union City School bell, from the late nineteenth century, is also housed on the premises.
URL: *No website.*
CONTACT: uchistoricalsociety@yahoo.com • (517) 741-3125

UNIVERSITY CENTER

Marshall M. Fredericks Sculpture Museum

ADDRESS: 7400 Bay Rd., University Center, MI 48710
ADMISSION: Free. Donations accepted.
ACCESSIBILITY: Fully accessible.
DESCRIPTION: The museum features a unique collection of more than 200 sculptures that span the 70-year career of "America's Public Sculptor," Marshall M. Fredericks, as well as rotating artist exhibitions from around the world. Fredericks is known nationally and internationally for his impressive monumental figurative sculpture, public memorials, fountains, portraits, and medals.
URL: *www.marshallfredericks.org*
CONTACT: mfsm@svsu.edu • (989) 964-7125

WESTPHALIA

Westphalia Historical Society Museum

ADDRESS: 120 Main St., Westphalia, MI 48894
ADMISSION: Contact site.
ACCESSIBILITY: Fully accessible.
DESCRIPTION: Each museum season, the museum showcases a different aspect of local history. Whether it is military history or local artists on display, the rotating exhibits hold something for all ages. In addition, the museum has a permanent exhibit about Westphalia businesses that people can see to learn more about the area.
URL: *www.westphaliahistory.weebly.com*
CONTACT: westphalia1836@gmail.com • (989) 587-3843

Williamston Depot Museum

ADDRESS: 369 West Grand River Ave., Williamston, MI 48895
ADMISSION: Free. Donations accepted.
ACCESSIBILITY: Fully accessible.
DESCRIPTION: The museum has a nine-case exhibit that tells the story of Williamston, beginning with the Native Americans up to the present. There is a new American Legion exhibit honoring the men and women of Williamston who served professionally and several displays that change throughout the year. In addition, photographs of historic Williamston are on display and in the collection.
URL: *www.williamstonmuseum.org*
CONTACT: williamstondepot2013@gmail.com • (517) 996-0205

CENTRAL

EASTERN

SPONSORED IN PART BY

FORD HOUSE

EDSEL & ELEANOR

EASTERN REGION

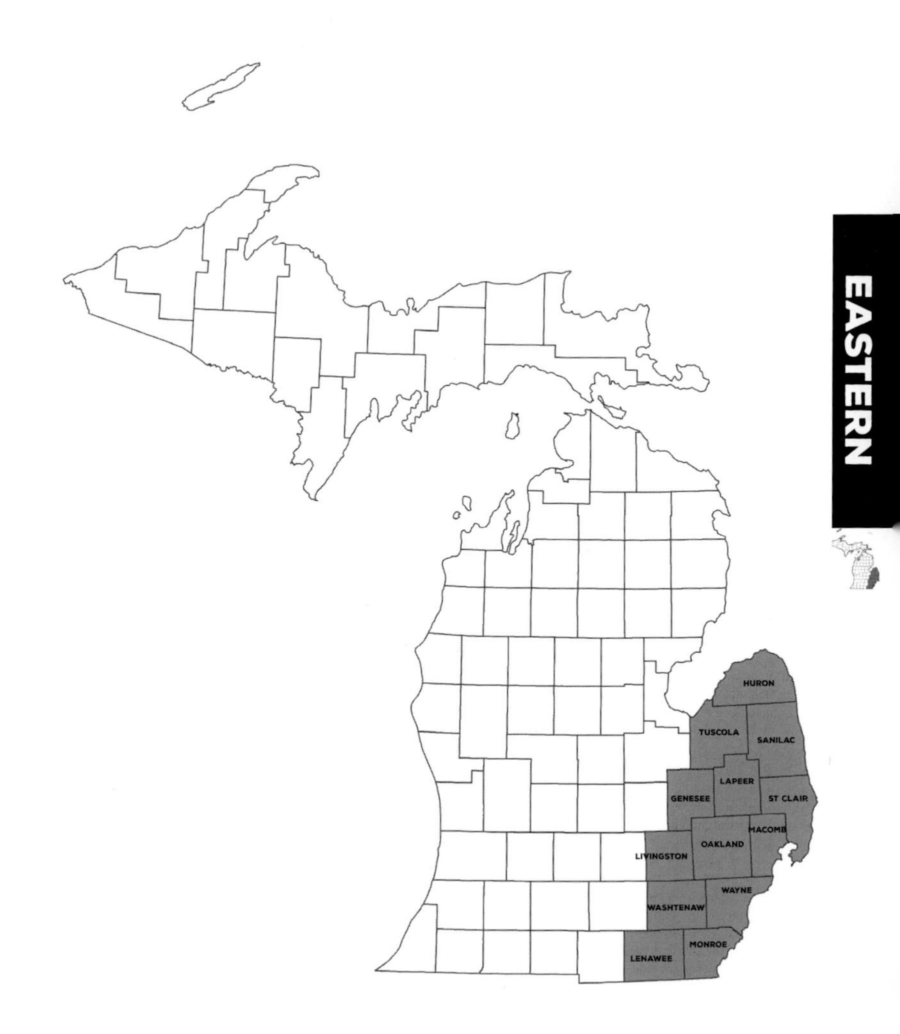

EASTERN

ADRIAN

Adrian Dominican Sisters

ADDRESS: 1257 E Siena Heights Dr., Adrian, MI 49221
ADMISSION: Contact site.
ACCESSIBILITY: Fully accessible.
DESCRIPTION: The historical display in Madden Hall is organized into three time periods: 1879 to 1933, 1933 to 1962, and 1963 to the present. Each contains narrative panels, photos, documents, and artifacts of its respective period. Also located within Madden Hall is the historic Holy Rosary Chapel, which was built 1905 to 1907.

URL: *www.adriandominicans.org*
CONTACT: jtobin@adriandominicans.org • (517) 266-3400

Lenawee County Historical Museum

ADDRESS: 110 E. Church St., Adrian, MI 49221
ADMISSION: Free. Donations accepted.
ACCESSIBILITY: Fully accessible.
DESCRIPTION: Exhibits in the museum feature the history of Lenawee County; its pioneers, railroads, industries; and other items linked to the county's history. The 100-year-old museum building is listed on the National Register of Historic Places and also includes an auditorium and a large archive of genealogical information.

URL: *www.lenaweehistoricalsociety.org*
CONTACT: lenaweemuseum@yahoo.com • (517) 265-6071

ALGONAC

Algonac-Clay Historical Society Museum

ADDRESS: 1240 St. Clair River Dr., Algonac, MI 48001
ADMISSION: Free. Donations accepted.
ACCESSIBILITY: Fully accessible.
DESCRIPTION: The Algonac-Clay Historical Society Museum features exhibits exploring the area's Native-American tribes, local churches, the military, and freighters. Aiming to preserve local historical artifacts and lore, the museum also houses a collection of school, city, and township memorabilia, and conducts historical research.

URL: *www.achistory.com*
CONTACT: achs@algonac-clay-history.com • (810) 794-9015

Maritime Museum

ADDRESS: 1117 St. Clair River Dr., Algonac, MI 48001
ADMISSION: Free. Donations accepted.
ACCESSIBILITY: Fully accessible.
DESCRIPTION: Algonac was the home of Chris-Craft Corporation, and the museum features full-size Chris-Craft boats along with Gar Wood boats and other boats from builders in area. Gar Wood's *Miss America X*, tall ship models, freighter models, and more than 10,000 other items are on display. There is a kids' room and a reference library.

URL: *www.achistory.com*
CONTACT: achs@algonac-clay-history.com • (810) 794-9015

Argus Museum

ADDRESS: 525 West William St., Ann Arbor, MI 48103
ADMISSION: Free. Donations accepted.
ACCESSIBILITY: Fully accessible.
DESCRIPTION: The Argus Museum is housed in the building where International Radio Corporation made radios, and its successor, Argus Cameras Inc., made photographic equipment. On display are Kadette radios, Argus cameras, prototypes, and extensive company archives. The Museum also hosts photography exhibitions by artists both in and outside of Ann Arbor.
URL: *www.argusmuseum.org*
CONTACT: director@argusmuseum.org • (734) 769-0770

Bentley Historical Library

ADDRESS: 1150 Beal Ave., Ann Arbor, MI 48109
ADMISSION: Free. Donations accepted.
ACCESSIBILITY: Fully accessible.
DESCRIPTION: The library contains a treasure trove of primary source material from the State of Michigan and the University of Michigan. Our research collections range from the official paperwork of governors, to the records of University of Michigan student and faculty life, to the entire state's historical archives of intercollegiate athletics, and much more.
URL: *www.bentley.umich.edu*
CONTACT: bentley.ref@umich.edu • (734) 764-3482

Judy & Stanley Frankel Detroit Observatory

ADDRESS: 1398 E. Ann St., Ann Arbor, MI 48109
ADMISSION: Free. Donations accepted.
ACCESSIBILITY: Partially accessible.
DESCRIPTION: Gaze into the past of our universe and the University of Michigan at the historic Detroit Observatory in Ann Arbor. Observe the stars through our 1857 Fitz Refracting telescope, learn about the history of astronomy, and experience a key site for the development of American science in the nineteenth century.
URL: *www.detroitobservatory.umich.edu*
CONTACT: detroit.observatory@umich.edu • (734) 763-2230

Gerald R. Ford Presidential Library

ADDRESS: 1000 Beal Ave., Ann Arbor, MI 48109
ADMISSION: Free. Donations accepted.
ACCESSIBILITY: Fully accessible.
DESCRIPTION: The Gerald R. Ford Library collects, preserves, and makes accessible to the public a rich body of archival materials on U.S. domestic issues, foreign relations, and political affairs during the Cold War era, focusing on the Ford administration. In addition to the permanent timeline exhibit on the lives of Gerald and Betty Ford, the library mounts several small temporary exhibits each year.
URL: *www.fordlibrarymuseum.gov*
CONTACT: ford.library@nara.gov • (734) 205-0555

Kempf House Museum

ADDRESS: 312 S. Division St., Ann Arbor, MI 48104
ADMISSION: Free. Donations accepted.
ACCESSIBILITY: Fully accessible.
DESCRIPTION: Displays in this 1853 Greek Revival house interpret Ann Arbor history and lifestyles from the late 1800s to the early 1900s. For most of its history, the house was owned by Reuben and Pauline Kempf, busy German-American music teachers. The restored rooms include the music studio, where the 1877 Steinway Concert Grand Piano remains as it has for more than 100 years.
URL: *www.kempfhousemuseum.org*
CONTACT: kempfhousemuseum@gmail.com • (734) 994-4898

Museum on Main Street

ADDRESS: 500 N. Main St., Ann Arbor, MI 48106
ADMISSION: Contact site.
ACCESSIBILITY: Fully accessible.
DESCRIPTION: The Museum on Main Street features changing exhibits that tell the various stories of Washtenaw County. Each exhibit focuses on a particular theme, story, or event. Exhibits have included photography, the Civil War, and how Washtenaw County's heritage is interpreted through local museums, historic homes and sites, and the programs and attractions they offer to the public.
URL: *www.washtenawhistory.org*
CONTACT: wchs-500@ameritech.net • (734) 662-9092

Sindecuse Museum of Dentistry

ADDRESS: 1011 N. University, G565 School of Dentistry, Ann Arbor, MI 48109
ADMISSION: Free. Donations accepted.
ACCESSIBILITY: Contact site.
DESCRIPTION: Visitors can view 13 exhibits focused on the history of Michigan and American dentistry at the only dental museum in the state. Cafe32, located next to the museum's main gallery, offers sandwiches, salads, premium coffees, and drinks. Exhibits may be explored before or after a snack or meal in the skylit gallery area.
URL: *www.sindecusemuseum.org*
CONTACT: dentalmuseum@umich.edu • (734) 763-0767

William L. Clements Library

ADDRESS: 909 S. University Ave., Ann Arbor, MI 48109
ADMISSION: Free. Donations accepted.
ACCESSIBILITY: Fully accessible.
DESCRIPTION: The library's mission is to collect, preserve, share, and promote the study of primary sources related to all aspects of the history and culture of North America, especially eighteenth- and nineteenth-century American history. Located on the University of Michigan's campus, it offers visitors the opportunity to view exhibits, attend programs, or make appointments for research.
URL: *www.clements.umich.edu*
CONTACT: clemdevcom@umich.edu • (734) 764-2347

BAD AXE

Bad Axe Museum of Local History

ADDRESS: 303 N. Port Crescent, Bad Axe, MI 48413
ADMISSION: Free. Donations accepted.
ACCESSIBILITY: Contact site.
DESCRIPTION: The museum is housed in a 1902 Dutch colonial home that was built by Wallace E. Allen, the town's longest-serving mayor. Owned by only one family, the museum is virtually the same structure it was originally. The museum depicts life at the turn of the century and is furnished with period antiques.
URL: *www.thehchs.org*
CONTACT: badaxehistorical@yahoo.com • (989) 550-2733

Pioneer Log Cabin Village

ADDRESS: 205 S. Hanselman St., Bad Axe, MI 48413
ADMISSION: Free. Donations accepted.
ACCESSIBILITY: Partially accessible.
DESCRIPTION: The Pioneer Log Cabin Village is the largest collection of authentically restored pioneer log buildings in Michigan. The six individual museums include a pioneer home, general store, one-room school, chapel, barn, and blacksmith shop. They were originally built between 1875 and 1900 and moved to this site from elsewhere around Huron County.
URL: *www.thehchs.org*
CONTACT: badaxehistorical@yahoo.com • (989) 550-2733

BELLEVILLE

Yankee Air Museum

ADDRESS: 47884 D St., Belleville, MI 48111
ADMISSION: Charge.
ACCESSIBILITY: Fully accessible.
DESCRIPTION: The museum educates and inspires visitors to embrace aviation's past as a vehicle to the future. Exhibits center on aviation in the twentieth century, local history of Willow Run, and hands-on activities for children. Come take a ride in one of the historic WWII-Era bombers—the B-17 *Yankee Lady* or the B-25 *Rosie's Reply* or our Vietnam-Era Huey helicopter!
URL: *www.yankeeairmuseum.org*
CONTACT: julie.osborne@yankeeairmuseum.org • (734) 483-4030

BIRMINGHAM

Birmingham Museum

ADDRESS: 556 W. Maple Rd., Birmingham, MI 48009
ADMISSION: Charge.
ACCESSIBILITY: Fully accessible.
DESCRIPTION: Two historic buildings from different eras set in a public park offer a multitude of experiences of Birmingham's story. The 1926 Allen House hosts changing exhibits and permanent displays, such as our immersive *CREEM Magazine* exhibit, while the 1822 Hunter House is the oldest house in Oakland County and reflects the pioneer days of settlement.
URL: *www.bhamgov.org/museum*
CONTACT: museum@bhamgov.org • (248) 530-1928

BRIGHTON

1885 Lyon One-Room Schoolhouse

ADDRESS: 11455 Buno Rd., Brighton, MI 48114
ADMISSION: Free. Donations accepted.
ACCESSIBILITY: Fully accessible.
DESCRIPTION: The Lyon One-Room Schoolhouse is a completely restored one-room school. The small museum highlights local memorabilia, including early veterinarian tools and early photos of Brighton. The school's interior setting is early 1900s. Beautiful maple top desks with the famous inkwell and flip-up bench seats. The Archive Room has family, business, and cemetery records.
URL: *www.brightonareahistorical.com*
CONTACT: info@brightonareahistorical.com • (810) 250-7276

City of Brighton Arts, Culture, and History (CoBACH) Center

ADDRESS: 202 W. Main St., Brighton, MI 48116
ADMISSION: Free. Donations accepted.
ACCESSIBILITY: Partially accessible.
DESCRIPTION: The free educational exhibits at the CoBACH Center change every two months. Visiting the museum is an excellent learning experience for both children and adults, who can explore the past and discuss how life, work, and home have changed. The CoBACH Center is in the original, two-story, 1879 brick firehouse in downtown Brighton.
URL: *www.brightonareahistorical.com*
CONTACT: info@brightonareahistorical.com • (810) 250-7276

1838 Old Village Cemetery

ADDRESS: 200 W. St. Paul St., Brighton, MI 48116
ADMISSION: Free. Donations accepted.
ACCESSIBILITY: Fully accessible.
DESCRIPTION: This outdoor museum of history is a walk into Brighton's past. Many names that appear on the gravestones are also found on street signs throughout the city and neighboring townships, including Governor Bingham's gravesite, Michigan's eleventh governor. There is a Self-Guided Walking Tour Booklet found inside a mailbox at the entrance for Civil War Veterans also buried here.
URL: *www.brightonareahistorical.com*
CONTACT: info@brightonareahistorical.com • (810) 250-7276

CANTON

Canton Historical Museum

ADDRESS: 1022 S Canton Center Rd., Canton, MI 48187
ADMISSION: Contact site.
ACCESSIBILITY: Fully accessible.
DESCRIPTION: Look back on the area's rural past at the one-room schoolhouse that serves as the Canton Historical Society's main museum. Historic artifacts and documents—including more than 60 pension and military records of Civil War soldiers—tell the history of the town from the Ice Age to the Nuclear Age.
URL: *www.cantonhistoricalsocietymi.org*
CONTACT: cantonhist@comcast.net • (734) 391-9352

Preservation Park

ADDRESS: 500 N Ridge Rd., Canton, MI 48187
ADMISSION: Contact site.
ACCESSIBILITY: Partially accessible.
DESCRIPTION: Preservation Park includes the Bartlett-Travis house and a white pole barn. The Bartlett-Travis House, once belonging to Canton families of those names, is a Victorian-style house built in the 1860s and "Victorianized" around 1900. The CHS Pole Barn, an agricultural museum, houses such things as old farm equipment, a 1920s kitchen, hand tools, a 1935 tractor, and corn shellers.
URL: *www.cantonhistoricalsocietymi.org*
CONTACT: cantonhist@comcast.net • (734) 397-0088

CASEVILLE

Historical Society of Caseville Museum

ADDRESS: 6733 Prospect St., Caseville, MI 48725
ADMISSION: Free. Donations accepted.
ACCESSIBILITY: Fully accessible.
DESCRIPTION: The Historical Society of Caseville maintains a museum in the 1890s building that once housed the local chapter of the Maccabees. Displays include fishing, farming, the lumber industry, school, and household exhibits. The society also has a collection of newspapers and yearbooks. Come to see the items and materials that illustrate the life, conditions, events, and activities of the past.
URL: *www.casevillemuseum.org*
CONTACT: chscm@comcast.net • (989) 856-9090

CASS CITY

Sanilac Petroglyphs Historic Site

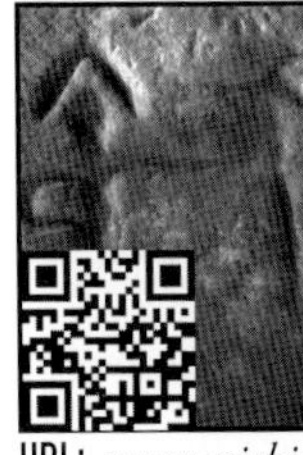

ADDRESS: 8251 Germania Rd., Cass City, MI 48726
ADMISSION: Recreation Passport required.
ACCESSIBILITY: Partially accessible.
DESCRIPTION: The park protects and interprets Michigan's largest known collection of early Native-American teachings carved in stone. The park is also a portion of the Cass River floodplain landscape with a mile-long self-guided walking trail. Admission is free with a Michigan State Parks Recreation Passport. The site is part of the Michigan History Center's Museum System.
URL: *www.michigan.gov/sanilacpetroglyphs*
CONTACT: mhcinfo@michigan.gov • (989) 856-4411

CHELSEA

Chelsea Area Historical Society & Museum

ADDRESS: 128 Jackson St., Chelsea, MI 48118
ADMISSION: Contact site.
ACCESSIBILITY: Fully accessible.
DESCRIPTION: The museum collects, manages, displays, and maintains local artifacts, archival information, photographs, genealogy records, and oral histories of citizens. In 2014, after years of transferring from temporary home to temporary home, the museum made its permanent move to a historic 1853 building on Jackson Street, opposite the Chelsea Train Depot.
URL: *www.chelseahistory.org*
CONTACT: president@chelseahistory.org • (734) 800-1850

CHESTERFIELD

Chesterfield Township Historical Village

ADDRESS: 47275 Sugarbush Rd., Chesterfield, MI 48047
ADMISSION: Free. Donations accepted.
ACCESSIBILITY: Fully accessible.
DESCRIPTION: The historical village has a one-room schoolhouse, working blacksmith shop, museum store, and log cabin. The village hosts many activities including reenactments, heritage festivals, antique car shows, weddings, and group tours. It is operated by the Chesterfield Township Historical Society, which maintains the Trinity Collection, dedicated to Chesterfield Township history.
URL: *www.chesterfieldhistoricalsociety.org*
CONTACT: chesterfieldhistory@yahoo.com • (586) 949-0400

Stahls Automotive Museum

ADDRESS: 56516 N. Bay Dr., Chesterfield, MI 48051
ADMISSION: Free. Donations accepted.
ACCESSIBILITY: Contact site.
DESCRIPTION: Stahls Automotive Museum helps visitors gain a better understanding of how the automobile developed from a novelty to a main form of transportation. In addition to the beautiful vintage cars on display, our collection also features gas pumps, road signs, oil cans, and other car-related accessories from the Depression Era.
URL: *www.stahlsauto.com*
CONTACT: info@stahlsauto.com • (586) 749-1078

CLAY TOWNSHIP

Log Cabin, DUR Wait Station, and Annex

ADDRESS: 4710 Point Tremble Rd., Clay Township, MI 48001
ADMISSION: Free. Donations accepted.
ACCESSIBILITY: Fully accessible.
DESCRIPTION: The log cabin presents life as it was in 1850 and displays artifacts donated by community members. The DUR Wait Station and section of tracks show where people waited for the interurban car from Detroit to Port Huron, and a small farm equipment exhibit is at the annex building. The site is open only upon request or for special events.
URL: *www.achistory.com*
CONTACT: achs@algonac-clay-history.com • (810) 794-9015

CLINTON TOWNSHIP

Albert L. Lorenzo Cultural Center

ADDRESS: 44575 Garfield Rd., Clinton Township, MI 48038
ADMISSION: Free. Donations accepted.
ACCESSIBILITY: Fully accessible.
DESCRIPTION: The center provides multidimensional cultural experiences in the areas of history, science, literature, current events, visual and performing arts, and popular culture. Each year, the center presents a themed anchor program and numerous presentations and displays that explore the influences and experiences that shape the community's heritage.
URL: *www.lorenzoculturalcenter.com*
CONTACT: culturalcenter@macomb.edu • (586) 445-7348

DAVISON

Davison Area Historical Museum

ADDRESS: 263 E. Fourth St., Davison, MI 48423
ADMISSION: Contact site.
ACCESSIBILITY: Partially accessible.
DESCRIPTION: Exhibits include toys, a dry goods store, a millinery shop, Davison's first post office, military uniforms, artifacts from area veterans, a scale of Davison Village as it was about 1903, and school artifacts. The Woolley Veterinarian Building is next to the museum. This local veterinary building has all its original medicines, equipment, and other artifacts.
URL: *www.davisonmuseum.org*
CONTACT: museumdavison@gmail.com • (810) 658-2286

Kitchen School

ADDRESS: 4010 S. State Rd., Davison, MI 48423
ADMISSION: Contact site.
ACCESSIBILITY: Partially accessible.
DESCRIPTION: This 150-year-old building is a one-room school as it would have appeared in 1940. It includes an outhouse, a wood stove, and playground equipment. Lumber dimensions and nail type were used to determine the age of the building. The school was named for Silas Kitchen, one of Davis Township's homesteaders.
URL: *www.davisonmuseum.org*
CONTACT: museumdavison@gmail.com • (810) 658-2286

Robert Williams Nature & Historical Learning Center

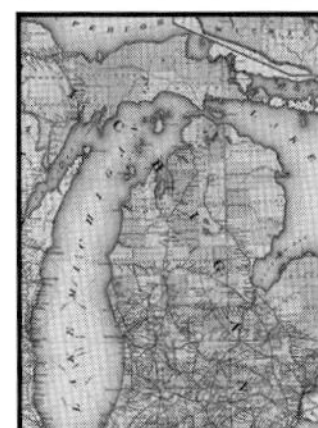

ADDRESS: 10069 Atherton Rd., Davison, MI 48423
ADMISSION: Contact site.
ACCESSIBILITY: Partially accessible.
DESCRIPTION: Visitors to the Robert Williams Nature & Historical Learning Center will enjoy information on Davison's first settlers and prominent individuals, including antique carriages and sleighs. Also available is a theater that seats 35 people.
URL: *No website.*
CONTACT: (810) 241-1810

DEARBORN

Henry Ford Museum of American Innovation

ADDRESS: 20900 Oakwood Blvd., Dearborn, MI 48124
ADMISSION: Charge.
ACCESSIBILITY: Fully accessible.
DESCRIPTION: The Henry Ford Museum of American Innovation showcases exhibits on transportation, technology, agriculture, industry, domestic life, public life, design, and decorative arts. Items big and small that have changed the world are the focus of the museum. For an additional fee, visitors can experience Greenfield Village, Ford Rouge Factory Tour, and the Giant Screen Experience.
URL: *www.thehenryford.org*
CONTACT: info@thehenryford.org • (313) 982-6001

Greenfield Village

ADDRESS: 20900 Oakwood Blvd., Dearborn, MI 48124
ADMISSION: Charge.
ACCESSIBILITY: Fully accessible.
DESCRIPTION: Greenfield Village is an outdoor experience that includes more than 80 authentic historic structures spread across more than 80 acres. Visitors can walk through Thomas Edison's Menlo Park laboratory and the courthouse where Abraham Lincoln practiced law. Jump aboard a Model T or take a ride on a steam-powered locomotive. Greenfield Village has something for everyone!
URL: *www.thehenryford.org*
CONTACT: info@thehenryford.org • (313) 982-6001

Ford Rouge Factory Tour

ADDRESS: 20900 Oakwood Blvd., Dearborn, MI 48124
ADMISSION: Charge.
ACCESSIBILITY: Fully accessible.
DESCRIPTION: The Ford Rouge Factory Tour allows visitors to walk through a working truck plant and view a gallery of Ford vehicles produced at the factory. There are two theater experiences available to visitors. Observation decks above the factory floor allow visitors to watch production of Ford trucks. Check the website for non-production dates.
URL: *www.thehenryford.org*
CONTACT: info@thehenryford.org • (313) 982-6001

McFadden-Ross House & Gardner House

ADDRESS: 915 S. Brady St., Dearborn, MI 48124
ADMISSION: Contact site.
ACCESSIBILITY: Contact site.
DESCRIPTION: The Gardner House, which once belonged to a childhood friend of Henry Ford, has three rooms and is Dearborn's oldest building located outside of Greenfield Village at The Henry Ford. The McFadden-Ross House has a variety of photos, papers, and books. In addition, visitors can explore exhibits and an archive with genealogical resources.
URL: *www.thedhm.com*
CONTACT: museum@ci.dearborn.mi.us • (313) 565-3000

Commandant's Quarters

ADDRESS: 21950 Michigan Ave., Dearborn, MI 48124
ADMISSION: Contact site.
ACCESSIBILITY: Contact site.
DESCRIPTION: Built in 1833, the Commandant's Quarters was one of eleven buildings that were part of the Detroit Arsenal at Dearborn. The period rooms in the building reflect how the commandants and their families would have lived during the Civil War. In addition, a selection of Civil War memorabilia and material is on display at the house.
URL: *www.thedhm.com*
CONTACT: museum@ci.dearborn.mi.us • (313) 565-3000

Detroit Historical Museum

ADDRESS: 5401 Woodward Ave., Detroit, MI 48202
ADMISSION: Charge.
ACCESSIBILITY: Partially accessible.
DESCRIPTION: The Detroit Historical Museum has many signature exhibits, plus changing exhibits, that allow visitors to explore more than 300 years of the city's history. The Streets of Old Detroit allow guests to "walk" through history and learn about industrial, sports, and domestic life. Visitors can explore the impact of Detroiters around the world in the Gallery of Innovation or Legends Plaza.
URL: *www.detroithistorical.org*
CONTACT: (313) 833-1805

Dossin Great Lakes Museum

ADDRESS: 100 Strand Dr. Belle Isle, Detroit, MI 48207
ADMISSION: Charge.
ACCESSIBILITY: Partially accessible.
DESCRIPTION: Located on Belle Isle, the museum emphasizes Detroit's role in regional and national maritime history through exciting exhibits like the *Miss Pepsi* hydroplane and ship models from one of the largest known collections of scale model ships in the world. Also on site are a bow anchor from the S.S. *Edmund Fitzgerald* and the William Clay Ford pilothouse.
URL: *www.detroithistorical.org*
CONTACT: (313) 833-1805

Ford Piquette Avenue Plant Museum

ADDRESS: 461 Piquette Ave., Detroit, MI 48202
ADMISSION: Charge.
ACCESSIBILITY: Fully accessible.
DESCRIPTION: The Ford Piquette Avenue Plant Museum is one of the oldest surviving automobile factories in the world. Opened in 1904 and the birthplace of the Model T, this U.S. National Historic Landmark is dedicated to interpreting and celebrating Detroit's automotive heritage and spirit of innovation. Visitors can enjoy guided tours, films, exhibits, and more than 60 rare vehicles.
URL: *www.fordpiquetteplant.org*
CONTACT: piquetteplant@gmail.com • (313) 872-8759

Hellenic Museum of Michigan

ADDRESS: 67 E. Kirby St., Detroit, MI 48202
ADMISSION: Free. Donations accepted.
ACCESSIBILITY: Partially accessible.
DESCRIPTION: The museum strives to share the struggles, triumphs, and contributions of the vibrant Greek immigrant community not only in Detroit but across the state of Michigan as well. The museum's collection shares the richness of Hellenic heritage and culture through its displays of Greek-American musical instruments, paintings, photographs, period clothing, pottery, and artwork.
URL: *www.hellenicmi.org*
CONTACT: hellenicmi@gmail.com • (313) 871-4100

Motown Historical Museum

ADDRESS: 2648 W. Grand Blvd., Detroit, MI 48208
ADMISSION: Charge.
ACCESSIBILITY: Fully accessible.
DESCRIPTION: The Motown Museum is one of Southeast Michigan's most popular tourist destinations. Visitors come from across America and throughout the world to stand in Studio A, where their favorite artists and groups recorded much-loved music and to view the restored upper flat where Berry Gordy lived with his young family during the company's earliest days.
URL: *www.motownmuseum.org*
CONTACT: info@motownmuseum.org • (313) 875-2264

Charles H. Wright Museum of African American History

ADDRESS: 315 E Warren Ave., Detroit, MI 48201
ADMISSION: Charge.
ACCESSIBILITY: Fully accessible.
DESCRIPTION: The Charles H. Wright Museum of African American History is the world's-largest institution dedicated to the African-American experience. Visitors can explore early civilizations in Africa, the tragedy of the middle passage and horrors of slavery, stories of courage along the Underground Railroad, and more.
URL: *www.thewright.org*
CONTACT: info@thewright.org • (313) 494-5800

Workers Row House

ADDRESS: 1430 Sixth St., Detroit, MI 48226
ADMISSION: Contact site.
ACCESSIBILITY: Contact site.
DESCRIPTION: The Workers Row House, one of the Detroit's oldest surviving structures, has been renovated and maintained by the Corktown Experience. The organization is a historic cultural center for Corktown and the Greater Detroit community. Visitors can choose to participate in tours, exhibits, plays, lectures, readings, video displays, meetings, cooking demonstrations, and craft making.
URL: *www.workersrowhouse.com*
CONTACT: corktownworkersrowhouse@gmail.com • (248) 224-4211

DEXTER

Dexter Area Historical Museum

ADDRESS: 3443 Inverness St., Dexter, MI 48130
ADMISSION: Free. Donations accepted.
ACCESSIBILITY: Contact site.
DESCRIPTION: The Dexter Area Historical Society was formed in 1971 to preserve and protect the history of the village of Dexter and the surrounding townships. Its main museum—containing a display area, genealogical and local history collection, and gift shop—resides within the circa 1883 St. Andrew's Church, which was moved to its current location in 1974.
URL: *www.dexterhistory.org*
CONTACT: dexmuseum@aol.com • (734) 426-2519

Gordon Hall

ADDRESS: 8341 Island Lake Rd., Dexter, MI 48130
ADMISSION: Contact site.
ACCESSIBILITY: Contact site.
DESCRIPTION: Historic Gordon Hall, built in the 1840s in southeastern Michigan, is owned and operated by the Dexter Area Historical Society. The society puts on events at Gordon Hall throughout the year to raise funds for the rehabilitation of the building. The building may also be rented for weddings and other events.

URL: *www.dexterhistory.org*
CONTACT: dexmuseum@aol.com • (734) 426-2519

Webster Historical Village

ADDRESS: 5583 Webster Church Rd., Dexter, MI 48130
ADMISSION: Contact site.
ACCESSIBILITY: Contact site.
DESCRIPTION: The society maintains a collection of historical buildings located in an area known locally as the "Webster Historical Village." Buildings include the Wheeler Wheelwright & Blacksmith Shop, Webster Old Township Hall, Podunk School, May's Old North Barn, and Crossroads Community Center. Most of the buildings have been moved to the site and restored.

URL: *www.webstertownshiphistoricalsociety.org*
CONTACT: wthsmi@gmail.com • (734) 368-0887

DUNDEE

Old Mill Museum

ADDRESS: 242 Toledo St., Dundee, MI 48131
ADMISSION: Free. Donations accepted.
ACCESSIBILITY: Fully accessible.
DESCRIPTION: The three-story Greek Revival mill built in 1848 features three floors of artifacts and exhibits chronicling local history. Visitors learn about the Ford Village Industries, farm and small town life in the nineteenth century, and Native-American life on the Macon Reserve.

URL: *www.dundeeoldmill.com*
CONTACT: museum@dundeeoldmill.com • (734) 529-8596

EASTPOINTE

Michigan Military Technical & Historical Society

ADDRESS: 16600 Stephens, Eastpointe, MI 48021
ADMISSION: Charge.
ACCESSIBILITY: Fully accessible.
DESCRIPTION: The Michigan Military Technical & Historical Society is dedicated to preserving the stories of Michigan citizens who served and sacrificed—both here and abroad—from WWI to the present. The 11,000-square-foot museum exhibits the equipment, weapons, uniforms, and other artifacts that bore witness to the high cost of freedom.

URL: *www.mimths.org*
CONTACT: mimths@mimths.org • (586) 872-2581

ELKTON

Elkton Area Historical Society

ADDRESS: 4910 York St., Elkton, MI 48731
ADMISSION: Contact site.
ACCESSIBILITY: Partially accessible.
DESCRIPTION: The Elkton Area Historical Society brings together and makes available the collection and display of material that helps establish or illustrate the area's history. The society maintains the 1865 Mayhew Log Cabin and Blacksmith Barn. Attractions include a 1916 80-horsepower Case stationary-type steam engine, farm-related artifacts, displays of memorabilia, and items of local interest.
URL: *www.thehchs.org/elkton*
CONTACT: phellwig2603@gmail.com • (989) 550-2603

FARMINGTON

Governor Warner Mansion

ADDRESS: 33805 Grand River Ave., Farmington, MI 48335
ADMISSION: Contact site.
ACCESSIBILITY: Contact site.
DESCRIPTION: This site is a Victorian home that shares the story of Farmington and the Warner family from 1867 to 1911. Visitors can also enjoy the extensive garden and the carriage house includes a classroom, nineteenth-century tools, and an early twentieth-century printing press and loom. At time of publication, the museum is closed for repairs so contact site for current information.
URL: *www.ci.farmington.mi.us/Community/Parks-and-Recreation/Warner-Mansion.aspx*
CONTACT: veedubbr@gmail.com • (248) 474-5500

FARMINGTON HILLS

Zekelman Holocaust Center (The HC)

ADDRESS: 28123 Orchard Lake Rd., Farmington Hills, MI 48334
ADMISSION: Charge.
ACCESSIBILITY: Fully accessible.
DESCRIPTION: Museum and Library Archive staff strive to engage, educate, and empower visitors to learn invaluable lessons from the past by remembering the Holocaust. Exhibits include artifacts, such as a Holocaust-era boxcar, video testimonies, films, paintings, and a sapling from the tree that grew outside Anne Frank's hiding place in Amsterdam.
URL: *www.holocaustcenter.org*
CONTACT: info@holocausetcenter.org • (248) 553-2400

FENTON

A.J. Phillips Fenton Museum

ADDRESS: 310 S. Leroy St., Fenton, MI 48430
ADMISSION: Contact site.
ACCESSIBILITY: Fully accessible.
DESCRIPTION: The Fenton Historical Society maintains the A.J. Phillips Fenton Museum in the personal office of A.J. Phillips, who owned a factory that made wooden snow shovels, ironing boards, screen windows, and doors. Exhibits include wars that Fenton residents served in, school memorabilia, and items that once belonged to Phillips.
URL: *www.fentonmihistory.com*
CONTACT: fhsmuseum@gmail.com • (810) 629-2570

FERNDALE

Ferndale Historical Society

ADDRESS: 1651 Livernois St., Ferndale, MI 48220
ADMISSION: Contact site.
ACCESSIBILITY: Partially accessible.
DESCRIPTION: The Ferndale Historical Museum is housed in a building given to the city by Canadian Legion Post No. 71. Collections date from the 1800s to the present and include a large military installation covering all of America's greatest wars, histories of all 8,000 structures in Ferndale, and local historical and genealogical information.
URL: *www.ferndalehistoricalsociety.org*
CONTACT: info@ferndalehistoricalsociety.org • (248) 545-7606

FLINT

Applewood Estate

ADDRESS: 1400 E Kearsley St., Flint, MI 48503
ADMISSION: Free. Donations accepted.
ACCESSIBILITY: Fully accessible.
DESCRIPTION: Built in 1916, Applewood is the historic family home and gentleman's farm of automotive pioneer and philanthropist Charles Stewart Mott. Applewood includes the main house, garage, barn, chicken coop, and gardener's cottage. Open seasonally to the public, the estate consists of an orchard, formal gardens, and demonstration garden—planted to bloom from spring to fall.
URL: *www.applewood.org*
CONTACT: ApplewoodInfo@ruthmott.org • (810) 233-3835

Genesee County Historical Society

ADDRESS: 316 Water St., Flint, MI 48503
ADMISSION: Contact site.
ACCESSIBILITY: Fully accessible.
DESCRIPTION: Since 1915, the Genesee County Historical Society (GCHS) has preserved meaningful historical artifacts and sites for the people throughout Genesee County. Located in the restored Durant-Dort offices, the birthplace of the General Motors Corporation, GCHS's headquarters is a National Historic Landmark that features photo exhibits, carriages, and furniture.
URL: *www.geneseehistory.org*
CONTACT: geneseecountyhistoricalsociety@gmail.com • (810) 410-4605

Longway Planetarium

ADDRESS: 1310 E. Kearsley St., Flint, MI 48503
ADMISSION: Charge.
ACCESSIBILITY: Fully accessible.
DESCRIPTION: The planetarium is used for school field trips but also provides public shows, family science workshops, and community events. The site has been recently renovated and gives visitors the opportunity to explore the universe. The museum provides live discussions and immersive virtual journeys to help visitors study history and science.
URL: *www.sloanlongway.org*
CONTACT: longway@sloanlongway.org • (810) 237-3400

Sloan Museum of Discovery

ADDRESS: 1221 E. Kearsley St., Flint, MI 48503
ADMISSION: Charge.
ACCESSIBILITY: Fully accessible.
DESCRIPTION: Four interactive galleries feature science and history in the new Sloan Museum of Discovery! Hagerman Street Early Childhood Learning gallery is an interactive child-sized neighborhood. The History Gallery features regional history and historical vehicles. The Discovery Hall Science Gallery teaches science with fun, hands-on exhibits.
URL: *www.sloanlongway.org*
CONTACT: sloan@sloanlongway.org • (810) 237-3450

Stockton Center at Spring Grove

ADDRESS: 720 Ann Arbor St., Flint, MI 48503
ADMISSION: Charge.
ACCESSIBILITY: Partially accessible.
DESCRIPTION: The elegantly restored Stockton House was built in 1872 by Colonel Stockton of the 16th Michigan Infantry. Displays include information on the Stockton family, Civil War history, and the original St. Joseph's hospital. Natural spring and Victorian gardens on the grounds are maintained by museum staff and are a great space for exploration and contemplation.
URL: *www.stocktonhousemuseum.com*
CONTACT: freemantgreer@gmail.com • (810) 882-1681

FLUSHING

Flushing Area Historical Society

ADDRESS: 431 West Main St., Flushing, MI 48433
ADMISSION: Free. Donations accepted.
ACCESSIBILITY: Fully accessible.
DESCRIPTION: The Flushing Area Historical Society maintains and operates the Flushing Depot as a museum and cultural center. The restored 1888 Grand Trunk depot museum features railroading and local history, veterinary medical equipment, drugstore items, 1930s kitchen appliances, and a shaving-mug display.
URL: *Facebook: Flushing Area Historical Society Museum*
CONTACT: fahs@att.net • (810) 487-0814

FRANKLIN

Franklin Historical Museum

ADDRESS: 26165 Thirteen Mile Rd., Franklin, MI 48025
ADMISSION: Free. Donations accepted.
ACCESSIBILITY: Fully accessible.
DESCRIPTION: The Franklin Historical Society preserves and protects objects, sites, and buildings connected to the history of Franklin, with archive topics ranging from archeological digs to village records. Housed in a 1951 ranch home, the Franklin Historical Museum contains artifacts related to Franklin's schools, businesses, government, and people. The museum is open by appointment.
URL: *www.franklin-history.org*
CONTACT: info@franklin-history.org • (248) 538-0273

GRAND BLANC

Heritage Museum

ADDRESS: 203 E. Grand Blanc Rd., Grand Blanc, MI 48439
ADMISSION: Free. Donations accepted.
ACCESSIBILITY: Fully accessible.
DESCRIPTION: Visit the Heritage Museum to learn stories from over two centuries of Grand Blanc's people, communities, and institutions. Located in the 1885 First Congregational Church building, the museum features exhibits on Native-American artifacts, agriculture, domestic life, mechanical music, education, and more.
URL: *www.cityofgrandblanc.com/city_services/heritage_museum.php*
CONTACT: gbhamuseum@gmail.com • (810) 694-7274

GROSSE ILE

Grosse Ile North Channel Light

ADDRESS: Lighthouse Point Rd., Grosse Ile, MI 48138
ADMISSION: Contact site.
ACCESSIBILITY: Contact site.
DESCRIPTION: Constructed in 1894 and redesigned in 1906, the North Channel Light is the only remaining lighthouse on Grosse Ile. The octagonal white tower stands at 40 feet tall and is under the protection of the Grosse Ile Historical Society. Tours share the history of the light and its importance to the area.
URL: *www.gihistsoc.org*
CONTACT: gihistsoc@gmail.com • (734) 675-1250

Michigan Central Railroad Depot Museum & Customs House

ADDRESS: 25020 E. River Rd., Grosse Ile, MI 48138
ADMISSION: Contact site.
ACCESSIBILITY: Contact site.
DESCRIPTION: The Michigan Central Depot Museum & Customs House features displays on railroad, community life, and significant Grosse Ile artifacts. The 1870s Customs House was moved back to its original location just behind the depot in 1979, greatly expanding the Grosse Ile Historical Society's meeting and museum facilities.
URL: *www.gihistsoc.org*
CONTACT: gihistsoc@gmail.com • (734) 675-1250

Naval Air Station GI Museum

ADDRESS: 9601 Groh Rd., Grosse Ile, MI 48138
ADMISSION: Contact site.
ACCESSIBILITY: Fully accessible.
DESCRIPTION: Located in the lobby of the Grosse Ile Township Hall, the Naval Air Station GI Museum has exhibits that focus on naval history and Grosse Ile's legacy as a Naval Air Station through artifacts and photographs. Also on- ite is a memorial garden.
URL: *www.gihistsoc.org*
CONTACT: gihistsoc@gmail.com • (734) 675-1250

GROSSE POINTE SHORES

Ford House

ADDRESS: 1100 Lake Shore Rd., Grosse Pointe Shores, MI 48236
ADMISSION: Charge.
ACCESSIBILITY: Partially accessible.
DESCRIPTION: Visitors can tour the historic home of automotive pioneer Edsel Ford and his family. Collections include paintings, graphic arts, French and English period furniture, glass, ceramics, and historical textiles. Permanent exhibits include the historic garage with Ford family vehicles. Changing exhibits occur throughout the year. Visitors can also enjoy the gardens and grounds of the house.
URL: *www.fordhouse.org*
CONTACT: info@fordhouse.org • (313) 884-4222

HADLEY

Hadley Mill Museum

ADDRESS: 3633 Hadley Rd., Hadley, MI 48440
ADMISSION: Free. Donations accepted.
ACCESSIBILITY: Contact site.
DESCRIPTION: Part of Hartwig Community Park, the Hadley Mill Museum is located in a historic 1874 gristmill and features a turbine, chutes, grain elevators, a line shaft, and a large engine. The three-story museum also houses numerous artifacts—allowing visitors to explore Hadley Township's past.
URL: *www.hadleytownship.org*
CONTACT: hadleyhistorical@gmail.com • (810) 797-4302

HAMBURG

Hamburg Township Museum

ADDRESS: 7225 Stone St., Hamburg, MI 48139
ADMISSION: Charge.
ACCESSIBILITY: Fully accessible.
DESCRIPTION: Established in 2004, the Hamburg Township Museum preserves and presents the history of Hamburg and the surrounding area through local history displays, active research archives, and changing special exhibits. The museum is located in one of Hamburg's most historic buildings, erected in 1865 as a Methodist place of worship.
URL: *www.hamburgmuseum.org*
CONTACT: info@hamburgmuseum.org • (810) 986-0190

HAMTRAMCK

Detroit History Club

ADDRESS: 3103 Commor, Hamtramck, MI 48212
ADMISSION: Charge.
ACCESSIBILITY: Partially accessible.
DESCRIPTION: The Detroit History Club is focused on history education in the most accessible, fun, and creative way possible. The club offers award-winning, highly curated, expertly led historical dinners, intimate concerts, lectures, and presentations, as well as themed game nights and adventures. All events and tours must be pre-booked via our website ticketing. Prices vary.
URL: *www.detroithistorytours.com*
CONTACT: office@detroithistorytours.com • (313) 539-7377

Hamtramck Historical Museum

ADDRESS: 9525 Jos. Campau, Hamtramck, MI 48212
ADMISSION: Free. Donations accepted.
ACCESSIBILITY: Fully accessible.
DESCRIPTION: The museum emphasizes interpretation of historical items from twentieth-century immigrants of Hamtramck—one of the most diverse cities in the nation. The collection ranges from documents and belongings to the items acquired in their new country to survive and thrive. Immigrant accomplishments also are highlighted to create a rich portrait of these new Americans.
URL: *www.hamtramckhistory.com*
CONTACT: hamtramckhistory@gmail.com • (313) 262-6571

HARBOR BEACH

Frank Murphy Memorial Museum

ADDRESS: 142 S. Huron Ave., Harbor Beach, MI 48441
ADMISSION: Contact site.
ACCESSIBILITY: Contact site.
DESCRIPTION: Learn about the impact and legacy of Frank Murphy at the museum dedicated to his life. He held many offices in the U.S. and the Philippines before his death as a sitting justice on the U.S. Supreme Court. Three of the five buildings on the site are open for tours, including a law office and family home.
URL: *www.harborbeach.com/frank-murphy-memorial-museum*
CONTACT: cityofharborbeach@gmail.com • (989) 479-3363

HARSENS ISLAND

Harsens Island Historical Museum

ADDRESS: 3058 S. Channel Dr., Harsens Island, MI 48028
ADMISSION: Contact site.
ACCESSIBILITY: Fully accessible.
DESCRIPTION: Museum visitors can view family trees of the island's founders; Great Lakes freighter models and live freighters; an operational steam whistle from the *J.B. Ford*; and special exhibits relating to Tashmoo Park, the old hotels, and the passenger steamer *Tashmoo*. The museum is run by the Harsens Island St. Clair Flats Historical Society.
URL: *www.harsensislandhistory.org*
CONTACT: xharpspah@aol.com • (734) 658-4502

HIGHLAND

Historic Edsel & Eleanor Ford Estate/Highland Recreation Area

ADDRESS: 5200 Highland Rd., Highland, MI 48357
ADMISSION: Contact site.
ACCESSIBILITY: Contact site.
DESCRIPTION: Enjoy visiting the former Ford family's "Haven Hill" estate, with beautiful acres of woods and trails, plus the three remaining historic structures currently being reconstructed: The Ford Gatehouse, Barn, & Carriage House. The site is accessible in the spring and summer. Park admission is free with a state of Michigan Recreation Passport.
URL: *www.fohravolunteers.org*
CONTACT: fohravolunteer@gmail.com • (248) 889-3750

HOLLY

Hadley House Museum

ADDRESS: 306 S Saginaw St., Holly, MI 48442
ADMISSION: Free. Donations accepted.
ACCESSIBILITY: Fully accessible.
DESCRIPTION: The Holly Historical Society organized in 1965 and acquired the 1873 Italianate Hadley House in 1986. The house has its original interior with period furniture and many rooms have historical displays. The museum also has a large local photographic collection and there is a carriage house still on the grounds.

URL: *www.hollyhistorical.org*
CONTACT: hollyhistoricalsoc@comcast.net • (248) 634-7946

HUDSON

Hudson Museum

ADDRESS: 219 W. Main St., Hudson, MI 49247
ADMISSION: Contact site.
ACCESSIBILITY: Partially accessible.
DESCRIPTION: The museum's collections are eclectic, but all help to tell the history of the Hudson area. Images, documents, and a section of original metal share the story of the development of the railroad. Manufacturing unique to the community is highlighted through exhibits related to Page Fence, Hardie Mfg. Co., and Bean Chamberlin Mfg. Co., to name a few.

URL: *www.hudsonmuseummi.weebly.com*
CONTACT: hudsonmuseum@d-pcomm.net • (517) 448-8858

William G. Thompson House Museum & Gardens

ADDRESS: 101 Summit St., Hudson, MI 49247
ADMISSION: Contact site.
ACCESSIBILITY: Fully accessible.
DESCRIPTION: The interior of the Thompson House Museum is filled to the brim with the collections of three generations of Thompsons, including oriental art, antiques, and paintings. The last owner, W. G. Thompson, was a collector of collections—focused on glass, porcelain and Asian art. The gardens provide year-round interest, set in the center of a city block.

URL: *www.wgthompsonmuseum.org*
CONTACT: ray.lennard@gmail.com • (517) 448-8125

IMLAY CITY

Imlay City Historical Museum

ADDRESS: 77 Main St., Imlay City, MI 48444
ADMISSION: Free. Donations accepted.
ACCESSIBILITY: Fully accessible.
DESCRIPTION: The museum is divided into thematic sections that transport visitors to different segments of the area's history. Whether it is a temporary special exhibit, the military display, memorabilia, or vignettes, one will have plenty to peruse. The museum honors the area's agricultural heritage with various displays in a separate annex building.

URL: *Facebook: Imlay City Museum*
CONTACT: ichistoricalmuseum@gmail.com • (810) 724-1904

LAPEER

Davis Brothers Farm Shop Museum

ADDRESS: 3520 Davis Lake Rd., Lapeer, MI 48446
ADMISSION: Contact site.
ACCESSIBILITY: Fully accessible.
DESCRIPTION: The Farm Shop Museum offers demonstrations of farming practices of the 1930s and 1940s, including the harvesting of grains, a working sawmill, blacksmith shop and lathe, and other exhibits and demonstrations. Take a peaceful walk through the Maple Sugar Bush Memorial Grove or belt of native white pines planted by Chatfield students.
URL: *www.lapeercountyhistoricalsociety.org*
CONTACT: LCHS.pobox72@gmail.com • (810) 245-0852

Lapeer County Heritage Museum

ADDRESS: 518 W. Nepessing St., Lapeer, MI 48446
ADMISSION: Free. Donations accepted.
ACCESSIBILITY: Contact site.
DESCRIPTION: At the Lapeer County Heritage Museum, exhibits are rotated and designed to introduce visitors to the people, events, and circumstances that shaped the history of the county. Notable individuals whose influence extended beyond the community are represented. Other exhibits explore logging, farming, state institutions, wars at home and abroad, and more.
URL: *www.lapeercountyhistoricalsociety.org*
CONTACT: LCHS.pobox72@gmail.com • (810) 245-5808

LINCOLN PARK

Lincoln Park Historical Museum

ADDRESS: 1335 Southfield Rd., Lincoln Park, MI 48146
ADMISSION: Free. Donations accepted.
ACCESSIBILITY: Fully accessible.
DESCRIPTION: The Lincoln Park Historical Society & Museum collects and preserves artifacts, including printed and photographic materials pertaining to the history of Lincoln Park, a neighboring community of Detroit. Built in the 1930s, the building served as a post office until 1991, when the historical society renovated and converted it to a museum.
URL: *www.lphistorical.org*
CONTACT: lpmuseum@gmail.com • (313) 386-3137

LIVONIA

Greenmead Historical Park

ADDRESS: 20501 Newburgh Rd., Livonia, MI 48152
ADMISSION: Free. Donations accepted.
ACCESSIBILITY: Fully accessible.
DESCRIPTION: Founded in 1956, the Livonia Historical Society helps fund Greenmead Historical Park, consisting of Greenmead Farm, the former homestead of Michigan pioneer Joshua Simmons; a 13-building historical village; a community garden; and more. The society also supports public programs, such as history lectures exploring topics of local interest.
URL: *www.livoniahistoricalsocietymi.org*
CONTACT: greenmead@livonia.gov • (248) 477-7375

MANCHESTER

John Schneider Blacksmith Shop

ADDRESS: 324 E Main St., Manchester, MI 48158
ADMISSION: Free. Donations accepted.
ACCESSIBILITY: Fully accessible.
DESCRIPTION: The John Schneider Blacksmith Shop is a complete shop with a working forge and tools of the trade. John Schneider was the last full-time blacksmith in Manchester. One of the last remaining intact "main street" blacksmith shops, the building houses and displays various local artifacts that have been collected by the Manchester Area Historical Society.
URL: *www.mahsmi.org*
CONTACT: info@mahsmi.org • Contact via website.

Kingsley-Jenter House

ADDRESS: 302 E. Main St., Manchester, MI 48158
ADMISSION: Free. Donations accepted.
ACCESSIBILITY: Fully accessible.
DESCRIPTION: The Kingsley-Jenter House is the headquarters for the Manchester Area Historic Society and serves as a community meeting place. The museum houses artifacts, archives, and a research facility. Several historical-themed meetings and events are held there throughout the year.
URL: *www.mahsmi.org*
CONTACT: info@mahsmi.org • Contact via website.

MARINE CITY

Marine City Community Pride & Heritage Museum

ADDRESS: 405 South Main St., Marine City, MI 48039
ADMISSION: Contact site.
ACCESSIBILITY: Partially accessible.
DESCRIPTION: The museum provides information on local history and shipbuilding in the area and helps teachers educate students about their community. The museum building was originally constructed in 1847 by Eber Brock Ward to house the Newport Academy, run by his sister Emily Ward. Exhibits touch on shipbuilding, Americana, business, farming, and genealogy research.
URL: *www.marinecitymuseum.com*
CONTACT: marinecitymuseum@hotmail.com • (810) 765-5446

MARLETTE

Marlette Train Depot

ADDRESS: 3325 Main St., Marlette, MI 48453
ADMISSION: Charge.
ACCESSIBILITY: Fully accessible.
DESCRIPTION: The Marlette Historical Society has restored the Marlette Train Depot, which is on the Michigan State Register of Historic Sites. The museum rotates historical items on display according to season. View collections devoted to local businesses of the past, farming in the community, and local schools. The society runs an operating Lionel train and the ticket office to purchase a ride.
URL: *Facebook: Marlette Train Depot*
CONTACT: carleen10650@yahoo.com • (989) 635-2277

MILAN

Friend-Hack House Museum

ADDRESS: 775 County St., Milan, MI 48160
ADMISSION: Free. Donations accepted.
ACCESSIBILITY: Contact site.
DESCRIPTION: The Friend-Hack house is a 134-year-old Victorian farm home with an interesting history. Visitors to the home, listed on the National Register of Historic Places, will learn about the original owner of the home, Olive Friend, and the fraudulent means of obtaining funds to build the house. Come see the home that locals refer to as the "House that Sugar Built."
URL: *www.historicmilan.com*
CONTACT: rod@tglyph.com • (734) 439-1297

Old Fire Barn

ADDRESS: 153 East Main St., Milan, MI 48160
ADMISSION: Free. Donations accepted.
ACCESSIBILITY: Fully accessible.
DESCRIPTION: The old Milan Fire Barn was built in 1897 and served as a fire station until 1979. The building housed the fire department and some of the city's fire vehicles, including a 1938 Ford Fire Truck. Over time, it also housed the police department, a jail—which consisted of a single jail cell—and the city library.
URL: *www.historicmilan.com*
CONTACT: rod@tglyph.com • (734) 439-1297

MILFORD

Mary Jackson's Childhood Home

ADDRESS: 648 Canal St., Milford, MI 48381
ADMISSION: Contact site.
ACCESSIBILITY: Fully accessible.
DESCRIPTION: The home is full of memorabilia of Mary Jackson's life and is preserved to be just as it was when she lived there. Mary Jackson was best known as a stage, screen, and TV actress. Her home was willed to the Milford Historical Society after her passing in 2005.
URL: *www.milfordhistory.org*
CONTACT: milfordhistory@hotmail.com • (248) 685-7308

Milford Historical Museum

ADDRESS: 124 E. Commerce St., Milford, MI 48381
ADMISSION: Contact site.
ACCESSIBILITY: Fully accessible.
DESCRIPTION: Located in an 1853 Greek Revival home, the entire second floor of the Milford Historical Museum is a display that is furnished as a home would have been in the late Victorian Era, complete with a living room, dining room, kitchen, and bedroom from that period. Many of the furnishings in the display are items that were manufactured in Milford.
URL: *www.milfordhistory.org*
CONTACT: milfordhistory@hotmail.com • (248) 685-7308

MILLINGTON

Millington-Arbela Historical Museum

ADDRESS: 8534 State St., Millington, MI 48746
ADMISSION: Free. Donations accepted.
ACCESSIBILITY: Partially accessible.
DESCRIPTION: The Millington-Arbela Historical Museum is housed in a historically registered 1897 fieldstone building. Opened in 1995, the museum is filled with regularly updated displays relating to life in Millington and Arbela townships. Visitors can research information on area businesses, families, schools, and veterans.
URL: *www.millingtonarbelahistoricalsociety.wordpress.com*
CONTACT: millingtonarbelahistoricalsociety@hotmail.com • (989) 871-5508

MONROE

Johnson-Phinney House

ADDRESS: 22 West Second St., Monroe, MI 48161
ADMISSION: Free. Donations accepted.
ACCESSIBILITY: Contact site.
DESCRIPTION: Run by the Monroe County Historical Society, the house showcases original Phinney family furniture and two doctors' offices. There is a War of 1812 International Peace Memorial on the grounds. The society also helps to interpret the Eby Log Cabin at the Monroe County Fairgrounds, offering free living history programs and a display of early farm equipment.
URL: *www.monroecountyhistoricalsocietymi.org*
CONTACT: johnsonphinneybuilding22@gmail.com • Contact via website.

Monroe County Museum

ADDRESS: 126 S. Monroe St., Monroe, MI 48161
ADMISSION: Free. Donations accepted.
ACCESSIBILITY: Fully accessible.
DESCRIPTION: Housed in a stately former post office in downtown Monroe, the museum collects, preserves, and presents the cultural, social, and natural history of Michigan's second oldest county. Signature exhibits focus on Native culture, French-Canadian settlement, and Monroe County veterans. The museum also features a series of temporary and seasonal exhibits throughout the year.
URL: *www.monroecountymuseum.com*
CONTACT: history@monroemi.org • (734) 240-7780

River Raisin National Battlefield Park

ADDRESS: 333 N Dixie Hwy., Monroe, MI 48162
ADMISSION: Free. Donations accepted.
ACCESSIBILITY: Contact site.
DESCRIPTION: The River Raisin NBP preserves and interprets the January 1813 battles of the War of 1812. The Visitor Center includes a diorama of the River Raisin Settlement, a theater, and exhibits on Native Americans, French settlement, the battles of the River Raisin, and more. Make sure to visit the River Raisin Heritage Trail, a short drive from the visitor center.
URL: *www.nps.gov/rira*
CONTACT: Contact via website. • (734) 243-7136

River Raisin Territorial Park

ADDRESS: 3815 North Custer Rd., Monroe, MI 48162
ADMISSION: Contact site.
ACCESSIBILITY: Partially accessible.
DESCRIPTION: Located on the north bank of its namesake river, the park explores the region's role during Michigan's settlement and territorial eras. The Navarre-Anderson Trading Post and Navarre-Morris Cabin are accompanied by a replica 1790s barn, bake oven, and orchard to recreate a long lot farm.
URL: *www.co.monroe.mi.us/437/Territorial-Park*
CONTACT: history@monroemi.org • (734) 240-7780

Vietnam Veterans Memorial and Museum

ADDRESS: 1095 N Dixie Hwy., Monroe, MI 48161
ADMISSION: Free. Donations accepted.
ACCESSIBILITY: Fully accessible.
DESCRIPTION: The Vietnam Veterans Memorial and Museum at Heck Park is dedicated to the memory of the Monroe County veterans who served in the Vietnam War. The museum houses exhibits, models, military gear, and mementos from the conflict and serves as a place of reflection. The grounds are host to several memorials and static exhibits of Vietnam-Era military equipment.
URL: *www.co.monroe.mi.us/440/Vietnam-Veterans-Memorial-and-Museum*
CONTACT: glenn.podhola@dcma.mil • (734) 240-7780

MONTROSE

Montrose Historical & Telephone Pioneer Museum

ADDRESS: 144 East Hickory St., Montrose, MI 48457
ADMISSION: Free. Donations accepted.
ACCESSIBILITY: Fully accessible.
DESCRIPTION: The Montrose Historical & Telephone Pioneer Museum is home to one of the best collections of telephones and related items in the United States. In addition to an extensive collection of telephones, the museum also houses local history collections as well as a large genealogical database.
URL: *www.montrosemuseum.com*
CONTACT: staff@montrosemuseum.com • (810) 639-6644

MOUNT CLEMENS

Crocker House Museum

ADDRESS: 15 Union St., Mount Clemens, MI 48043
ADMISSION: Charge.
ACCESSIBILITY: Contact site.
DESCRIPTION: Step back in time to the late 1800s, when Mount Clemens was world-famous for its mineral baths. The Italianate-style Crocker House, once home to Mount Clemens' first mayors, now features exhibits about Victorian home life as well as local histories and industries. While you're here, be sure to visit the gift shop and enjoy a stroll through the gardens.
URL: *www.crockerhousemuseum.org*
CONTACT: info@crockerhousemuseum.org • (586) 465-2488

Michigan Transit Museum

ADDRESS: 200 Grand Ave., Mount Clemens, MI 48043
ADMISSION: Contact site.
ACCESSIBILITY: Partially accessible.
DESCRIPTION: One of the original Grand Trunk Railway stations, the Mount Clemens Depot originally opened for business on November 21, 1859. Today, it is home to the Michigan Transit Museum. Visitors can view full-size locomotives, freight cars, electric trolleys, and rapid transit cars. The museum also has a railroad-related archival collection.
URL: *www.michigantransitmuseum.com*
CONTACT: Contact via website. • (586) 463-1863

NEW BALTIMORE

Grand Pacific House Museum

ADDRESS: 51065 Washington St., New Baltimore, MI 48047
ADMISSION: Contact site.
ACCESSIBILITY: Contact site.
DESCRIPTION: The Grand Pacific House Museum is operated by the New Baltimore Historical Society, which strives to preserve all historical aspects of the Anchor Bay area. Originally built in 1881 for use as a hotel and later used as a boarding house and a soda fountain and candy store, the museum building now contains exhibits about New Baltimore's history.
URL: *www.newbaltimorehistorical.org*
CONTACT: (586) 725-4755

NORTHVILLE

Mill Race Village

ADDRESS: 215 Griswold St., Northville, MI 48167
ADMISSION: Free. Donations accepted.
ACCESSIBILITY: Partially accessible.
DESCRIPTION: The Northville Historical Society created Mill Race Village to share a small Victorian era village within a beautifully landscaped park. Some of the buildings that make up the village are the Cady Inn, a general store, Weaver's Cottage, Hirsch Blacksmith Shop, Interurban Station, and multiple homes. Descriptive signage is available along with picnic spots to enjoy with family and friends.
URL: *www.millracenorthville.org*
CONTACT: office@millracenorthville.org • (248) 348-1845

OAKLAND TOWNSHIP

Oakland Township Historical Society Museum

ADDRESS: 384 W Predmore Rd., Oakland Township, MI 48363
ADMISSION: Free. Donations accepted.
ACCESSIBILITY: Fully accessible.
DESCRIPTION: The Oakland Township Historical Society leases part of the 16-acre Cranberry Lake Farm Historic District in township-owned Cranberry Lake Park. The society's museum is in the tenant house and the archives are available for research on the second floor of the main house.
URL: *www.oaklandtownshiphistoricalsociety.org*
CONTACT: othspresident@gmail.com • (248) 651-7526

ONSTED

Wooden Old Stone School

ADDRESS: 11992 Stephenson Rd., Onsted, MI 49265
ADMISSION: Free. Donations accepted.
ACCESSIBILITY: Contact site.
DESCRIPTION: The Wooden Schoolhouse is a landmark of rural life in early Michigan. The school was built from stones from local farm fields in 1850, by Rev. Robert Wooden, local farmer and preacher. Come visit and take a glimpse into early school days in Michigan. Visit the website to learn more and view hours of operation.
URL: *www.woodenoldstoneschoolhouse.com*
CONTACT: woodenoldstoneschoolhouse@gmail.com • (517) 605-9787

ORCHARD LAKE

Orchard Lake Museum

ADDRESS: 3951 Orchard Lake Rd., Orchard Lake, MI 48323
ADMISSION: Free. Donations accepted.
ACCESSIBILITY: Contact site.
DESCRIPTION: Home of the Greater West Bloomfield Historical Society, the Orchard Lake Museum houses a collection of local artifacts, historical photos, documents, as well as hands-on exhibits for children. Items permanently on display include a seventeenth-century dugout canoe, the neon landmark Keego Cinema sign, and a working ticket machine.
URL: *www.gwbhs.org*
CONTACT: contact@gwbhs.org • (248) 757-2451

ORTONVILLE

Old Mill Museum

ADDRESS: 366 Mill St., Ortonville, MI 48462
ADMISSION: Contact site.
ACCESSIBILITY: Partially accessible.
DESCRIPTION: The museum is housed in a repurposed grist mill built in 1856 from hand-hewn timbers taken from the property. One floor is dedicated to military exhibits, from the Civil War to current conflicts. Another floor houses a 1920s fire truck, along with farming artifacts. Additional floors house smaller displays of donated artifacts by local families.
URL: *www.ochsoldmill.org*
CONTACT: ochsoldmill@gmail.com • (248) 793-1807

OTISVILLE

Otisville Museum

ADDRESS: 122 E. Main St., Otisville, MI 48463
ADMISSION: Free. Donations accepted.
ACCESSIBILITY: Fully accessible.
DESCRIPTION: The Otisville Area Museum project began in 2010. Now in full operation, the museum features a variety of displays on farming, the military, lumbering, Otisville sports, Otisville High School class composite pictures, and more. One unique artifact on display is a pair of elk antlers found in Otisville Lake—dated to around 1520.
URL: *Facebook: Otisville Museum*
CONTACT: oaha1982@yahoo.com • (810) 397-0453

PIGEON

Pigeon Historical Museum

ADDRESS: 59 South Main St., Pigeon, MI 48755
ADMISSION: Contact site.
ACCESSIBILITY: Fully accessible.
DESCRIPTION: The Pigeon Historical Museum, also known as The Depot Museum, occupies the former Pigeon Depot which was built in 1908 as a joint venture of the Pontiac, Oxford, and Northern and the Pere Marquette Railroads. The museum contains an impressive collection of more than 2,000 artifacts from past Pigeon businesses and the people who lived here.
URL: *www.pigeonhistoricalsociety.com*
CONTACT: pigeonhistorical@gmail.com • (989) 453-3242

PITTSFIELD TOWNSHIP

Historic Sutherland-Wilson Farm

ADDRESS: 797 W. Textile Rd., Pittsfield Township, MI 48103
ADMISSION: Contact site.
ACCESSIBILITY: Fully accessible.
DESCRIPTION: The museum is located in the Greek Revival home of Langford and Lydia Sutherland, who settled in Pittsfield Township in 1833. The museum showcases furniture from the 1830s–1900s, plat maps, newspaper clippings, and historical information about the township. Outbuildings consist of a barn, carriage house, icehouse, woodshed, and pump house.
URL: *www.pittsfieldhistory.org*
CONTACT: info@pittsfieldhistory.org • (734) 668-2607

PLYMOUTH

Jarvis Stone School Historic District

ADDRESS: 7991 North Territorial Rd., Plymouth, MI 48170
ADMISSION: Free. Donations accepted.
ACCESSIBILITY: Partially accessible.
DESCRIPTION: The Salem Area Historical Society operates the Jarvis Stone School Historic District—home to the South Salem Stone School and the Dickerson Barn. The 1857 school was in continuous use for 110 years. The barn—built in 1830—is the oldest timber-frame barn in Washtenaw County. The site also has five murals featuring nineteenth-century Salem structures.
URL: *www.sahshistory.org*
CONTACT: salem_area_hs@yahoo.com • (248) 486-0669

Plymouth Historical Museum

ADDRESS: 155 S. Main St., Plymouth, MI 48170
ADMISSION: Charge.
ACCESSIBILITY: Fully accessible.
DESCRIPTION: The museum gives it visitors the opportunity to explore America in the late nineteenth and early twentieth century. Two floors of exhibits include a re-creation of a Victorian Main Street, a large collection of Abraham Lincoln materials, and a Timeline of Plymouth, featuring displays of the Daisy Air Rifle Factory, Ford Village Industries, the Alter Motor Car and much more.
URL: *www.plymouthhistory.org*
CONTACT: secretary@plymouthhistory.org • (734) 455-8940

PONTIAC

Pine Grove

ADDRESS: 405 Cesar E. Chavez Ave., Pontiac, MI 48342
ADMISSION: Free. Donations accepted.
ACCESSIBILITY: Partially accessible.
DESCRIPTION: Pine Grove, home of the Oakland County Pioneer and Historical Society, is a collection of 10 buildings on 4.5 acres of land. Attractions include the Wisner mansion, a summer kitchen, an outhouse, a smokehouse, and a root cellar. Don't miss the Drayton Plains One-Room Schoolhouse and the carriage house, which is home to the research library and archives and the Pioneer Museum.
URL: *www.ocphs.org*
CONTACT: office@ocphs.org • (248) 338-6732

PORT AUSTIN

Port Austin History Center

ADDRESS: 1424 Pte. Aux Barques Rd., Port Austin, MI 48467
ADMISSION: Free. Donations accepted.
ACCESSIBILITY: Fully accessible.
DESCRIPTION: The site presents the history of Port Austin, Grindstone City, and Port Crescent. Exhibits depict early area industries; the Great Thumb Fire of 1881; Native Americans in the Thumb; and the Port Austin Reef Lighthouse. The grounds feature historic buildings, including a log cabin and log barn, a nineteenth-century Grindstone City house, and a 1950s barbershop.
URL: *Facebook: Port Austin Area Historical Society*
CONTACT: portaustinhistorycenter@gmail.com • (989) 551-5532

PORT HOPE

Pointe aux Barques Lighthouse

ADDRESS: 7320 Lighthouse Rd., Port Hope, MI 48468
ADMISSION: Charge.
ACCESSIBILITY: Contact site.
DESCRIPTION: Immerse yourself in lighthouse, lifesaving, and Huron County history. There are exhibits on lighthouse operations, area shipwrecks—including the 1966 wreck of the *Daniel J. Morrell*—and the Pointe aux Barques lifesaving station. On rotating display is the only sixteen-panel, Fresnel lens created for the Great Lakes and used at the lighthouse from 1873 to 1969.
URL: *www.pointeauxbarqueslighthouse.org*
CONTACT: pointeauxbarques@yahoo.com • (586) 243-1838

Port Hope Railroad Depot

ADDRESS: 8046 Portland Ave., Port Hope, MI 48468
ADMISSION: Contact site.
ACCESSIBILITY: Fully accessible.
DESCRIPTION: Located on the shore of Lake Huron, this historic train station preserves the heritage of the Port Hope community. Visitors can explore an authentic 1904 Pere Marquette railroad depot with interactive exhibits, view a model railroad, and hike along a walking trail.
URL: *www.porthopedepot.org*
CONTACT: porthopedepot@gmail.com • (517) 420-4147 or (989) 670-6200

Carnegie Center Museum

ADDRESS: 1115 6th St., Port Huron, MI 48060
ADMISSION: Charge.
ACCESSIBILITY: Fully accessible.
DESCRIPTION: The museum features more than 16,000 items focusing on the culture, art, and history of St. Clair County, with a portion of the collection dedicated specifically to Great Lakes maritime history. The Carnegie Museum preserves and illuminates the stories of Michigan and the Great Lakes, through the lives and experiences of local people.
URL: *www.phmuseum.org*
CONTACT: info@phmuseum.org • (810) 982-0891

Fort Gratiot Light Station

ADDRESS: 2802 Omar St., Port Huron, MI 48060
ADMISSION: Charge.
ACCESSIBILITY: Contact site.
DESCRIPTION: The Fort Gratiot Light Station, circa 1829, is the oldest lighthouse in Michigan and was re-opened to the public in 2012. The original structure was 65 feet tall but was extended to its present height of 82 feet in the early 1860s. Visitors need closed-toe shoes to climb to the top of the tower.
URL: *www.phmuseum.org*
CONTACT: info@phmuseum.org • (810) 982-0891

Huron Lightship

ADDRESS: 800 Prospect Pl., Port Huron, MI 48060
ADMISSION: Charge.
ACCESSIBILITY: Contact site.
DESCRIPTION: The Huron Lightship was a "floating lighthouse" and spent its entire career on the Great Lakes with 36 years in Port Huron. Retired in 1970, the ship has been refinished as a museum and traces the history of its service and those who served. There is a fog horn sounding on Memorial Day, Independence Day, and Labor Day.
URL: *www.phmuseum.org*
CONTACT: info@phmuseum.org • (810) 984-9768

Thomas Edison Depot Museum

ADDRESS: 510 Edison Pky., Port Huron, MI 48060
ADMISSION: Charge.
ACCESSIBILITY: Fully accessible.
DESCRIPTION: The Thomas Edison Depot is where a teenaged Thomas Edison worked during his years in Port Huron. A restored baggage car recreates his mobile chemistry lab, where some of his early experiments were conducted. The Black Mariah movie theater shows films about Edison, and there are also interactive displays and experiments.
URL: *www.phmuseum.org*
CONTACT: info@phmuseum.org • (810) 982-0891

PORT SANILAC

Sanilac County Historic Village & Museum

ADDRESS: 228 South Ridge St., Port Sanilac, MI 48469
ADMISSION: Charge.
ACCESSIBILITY: Partially accessible.
DESCRIPTION: Tour the beautiful Loop-Harrison Mansion, built in 1872. Enjoy our historic village, set on 10 acres with 17 historic buildings, a 1942 U.S. Troop Train, 14 lovely gardens, benches and swings, and a one-mile walking path and nature trail. Many on-site events are available throughout the year for people of all ages.

URL: *www.sanilaccountymuseum.org*
CONTACT: sanilacmuseum@gmail.com • (810) 622-9946

RICHMOND

Richmond Historic Village

ADDRESS: 36045 Park St., Richmond, MI 48062
ADMISSION: Free. Donations accepted.
ACCESSIBILITY: Fully accessible.
DESCRIPTION: The Richmond Historic Village consists of the Donley Cabin built in 1853, a one-room schoolhouse that was built in 1885, and the Columbus Train Depot. There is also a carriage house and a museum with displays that change bi-annually. Recently, a barn has been moved on site and restored. Come explore the past with us!

URL: *www.richmondhistoricalsociety.org*
CONTACT: rahgs2023@yahoo.com •

RIVES JUNCTION

Stewart Farm Museum

ADDRESS: 10138 Tompkins Rd., Rives Junction, MI 49277
ADMISSION: Free. Donations accepted.
ACCESSIBILITY: Fully accessible.
DESCRIPTION: The Tompkins Historical Stewart Farm Museum is a short drive off M-50 in Tompkins. The Stewart property features a farmhouse museum, rug looms and blacksmith demonstrations, a replica frontier log cabin, an 1880s schoolhouse, and a working windmill.

URL: *www.TompkinsCenterHistorical.org*
CONTACT: Tompkinshistorical@gmail.com • (517) 569-2100

ROCHESTER HILLS

Rochester Hills Museum at Van Hoosen Farm

ADDRESS: 1005 Van Hoosen Rd., Rochester Hills, MI 48306
ADMISSION: Charge.
ACCESSIBILITY: Fully accessible.
DESCRIPTION: Located in Stoney Creek Village, this 16-acre museum complex—featuring structures original to the property—was home to the Taylor and Van Hoosen families dating back to 1823. Presented in a restored 1927 dairy barn are well-designed, informative exhibits highlighting the settlement, agriculture, industry, and cultural evolution of the greater Rochester community.

URL: *www.rochesterhills.org/museum*
CONTACT: rhmuseum@rochesterhills.org • (248) 656-4663

ROMEO

Bancroft-Stranahan Museum

ADDRESS: 132 Church St., Romeo, MI 48065
ADMISSION: Contact site.
ACCESSIBILITY: Partially accessible.
DESCRIPTION: The 1868 Greek revival-style building that now contains the Bancroft-Stranahan Museum was formerly a home to the Bancroft and Stranahan families of Romeo. The museum has period settings including furniture, clothing, kitchenware, and changing displays, as well as a collection of oil paintings by William Gibbs.

URL: *www.romeohistoricalsociety.org*
CONTACT: rhs@romeohistoricalsociety.org • (586) 752-4111

Clyde Craig Blacksmith Shop Museum

ADDRESS: 301 N. Bailey St., Romeo, MI 48065
ADMISSION: Contact site.
ACCESSIBILITY: Partially accessible.
DESCRIPTION: In 1920, Clyde Craig opened a blacksmith, farrier, fur-trading station and veterinarian and wheelwright shop. When Craig died in 1970, the shop was moved and turned into a working blacksmith shop and museum. Using the 2,800-degree forge, smiths still use the old tools to shape metal, just as in the past.

URL: *www.romeohistoricalsociety.org*
CONTACT: rhs@romeohistoricalsociety.org • (586) 752-4111

Romeo Arts & Archives Center

ADDRESS: 290 N. Main St., Romeo, MI 48065
ADMISSION: Contact site.
ACCESSIBILITY: Contact site.
DESCRIPTION: The Romeo Arts & Archives Center is operated by the Romeo Historical Society, which seeks to preserve, document, and promote the history and heritage of the Village of Romeo and its surroundings. The Center contains archives and changing displays relating to Romeo's past, as well as a small research library for study—featuring oil paintings by William Gibbs.

URL: *www.romeohistoricalsociety.org*
CONTACT: rhs@romeohistoricalsociety.org • (586) 752-4111

ROSEVILLE

Leon Buyse Memorial Library and Museum

ADDRESS: 18740 E. Thirteen Mile Rd., Roseville, MI 48066
ADMISSION: Free. Donations accepted.
ACCESSIBILITY: Fully accessible.
DESCRIPTION: The Leon Buyse Memorial Library and Museum specializes in Flemish history. Among the collections are handmade lace samples; death memorial cards and obituaries; and the *Gazette Van Detroit*, in paper and microfilm. The Genealogical Society of Flemish Americans also holds the only copy of the *Gazette Van Moline* on microfilm.

URL: *www.flemishlibrary.org*
CONTACT: flemishlibrary@gmail.com • (586) 777-2720

ROYAL OAK

Royal Oak Historical Society Museum

ADDRESS: 1411 W. Webster, Royal Oak, MI 48073
ADMISSION: Free. Donations accepted.
ACCESSIBILITY: Fully accessible.
DESCRIPTION: Located inside the Royal Oak Historic Northwood Fire Station, the museum includes a collection of the archival history of the Royal Oak Fire Department and George Dondero's Lincoln collection. It features other rotating exhibits and items that focus on the founding families of Royal Oak and the impact of lumber barons on the area.
URL: *www.royaloakhistoricalsociety.org*
CONTACT: curator@royaloakhistoricalsociety.org • (248) 439-1501

SEBEWAING

Charles W. Liken Museum

ADDRESS: 325 N. Center, Sebewaing, MI 48759
ADMISSION: Free. Donations accepted.
ACCESSIBILITY: Contact site.
DESCRIPTION: The Charles W. Liken House is a Victorian house built in approximately 1880 by the town's founding father, John C. Liken. The home includes a collection of replicated versions of original furnishings. Other rooms showcase former businesses and vintage clothing. There is also a religious room, a child's bedroom, and a sewing room as well as vintage toys in the basement.
URL: *www.thehchs.org/sebewaing*
CONTACT: (989) 450-9394

Old Sebewaing Township Hall

ADDRESS: 92 S. Center St., Sebewaing, MI 48759
ADMISSION: Contact site.
ACCESSIBILITY: Partially accessible.
DESCRIPTION: The Old Sebewaing Township Hall features exhibits on printing, the fire department water tank, and Sebewaing Beer. The history of daily life in Sebewaing is shared through displays on the post office, township office, jail, and high school.
URL: *www.thehchs.org/sebewaing*
CONTACT: (989) 450-9394

SHELBY TOWNSHIP

Packard Proving Grounds Historic Site

ADDRESS: 49965 Van Dyke Ave., Shelby Township, MI 48317
ADMISSION: Free. Donations accepted.
ACCESSIBILITY: Partially accessible.
DESCRIPTION: The Packard Proving Grounds was an automotive testing site designed in part by Albert Kahn for the Packard Motor Car Company and in operation from 1928 to 1956 except during WWII. Today, the 17-acre site, along with many of the buildings, can be booked for large and small group tours as well as weddings and parties.
URL: *www.packardprovinggrounds.org*
CONTACT: packardprovinggrounds@gmail.com • (586) 739-4800

SOUTH LYON

Green Oak Township Heritage Museum

ADDRESS: 10789 Silver Lake Rd., South Lyon, MI 48178
ADMISSION: Contact site.
ACCESSIBILITY: Fully accessible.
DESCRIPTION: Organized in 1974, the Green Oak Township Historical Society maintains a heritage museum, featuring artifacts from the 1800s until today. The museum is located adjacent to the 1856 Green Oak Township Hall, which was restored by the society.

URL: *www.greenoaktownshiphistoricalsociety.org*
CONTACT: mfdharrington@gmail.com • (248) 446-0789

South Lyon Area Historical Society Historic Village

ADDRESS: 300 Dorothy St., South Lyon, MI 48178
ADMISSION: Contact site.
ACCESSIBILITY: Partially accessible.
DESCRIPTION: Visit the historic village maintained by the South Lyon Area Historical Society to see an early-nineteenth-century railroad depot, a caboose, gazebo, freight house, meeting hall, the 1907 Washburn School and a 1930s chapel. Guided tours are available of the village as well as special programs throughout the year.

URL: *www.slahs.net*
CONTACT: southlyonahs@gmail.com • (248) 437-9929

SOUTHFIELD

Mary Thompson Farmhouse

ADDRESS: 25630 Evergreen Rd., Southfield, MI 48076
ADMISSION: Contact site.
ACCESSIBILITY: Partially accessible.
DESCRIPTION: The farmhouse has furniture and belongings of Southfield teacher and benefactor Mary Thompson and Southfield's first councilwoman, Jean McDonnell. The house features post-and-beam construction, was built in 1840, and was renovated in the 1960s and 1970s.

URL: *www.southfieldhistoricalsociety.wordpress.com*
CONTACT: historicsouthfield@gmail.com

Town Hall Museum

ADDRESS: 26080 Berg Rd., Southfield, MI 48033
ADMISSION: Free. Donations accepted.
ACCESSIBILITY: Fully accessible.
DESCRIPTION: The Town Hall Museum has exhibits about the Potawatomi people living in our area, the Underground Railroad at the Southfield Reformed Presbyterian Church, local residents in World War I, and Harry Brooks, who was an early aviator for Henry Ford.

URL: *www.southfieldhistoricalsociety.wordpress.com*
CONTACT: historicsouthfield@gmail.com

ST. CLAIR

St. Clair Historical Museum and Research Center

ADDRESS: 308 S. 4th St., St. Clair, MI 48079
ADMISSION: Free. Donations accepted.
ACCESSIBILITY: Partially accessible.
DESCRIPTION: The St. Clair Historical Museum and Research Center features a model of Fort Sinclair, the Belle Reve Room with a 250-year-old oak fireplace, and specialty rooms displaying artifacts from local shipbuilding companies, shoe shops, nineteenth-century kitchens, salt production companies, and churches. Video displays tell of St. Clair's connection to other places in North America.
URL: *www.historicstclair.com*
CONTACT: historicstclair@gmail.com • (810) 329-6888

ST. CLAIR SHORES

Selinsky-Green Farmhouse Museum

ADDRESS: 22500 Eleven Mile Rd., St. Clair Shores, MI 48081
ADMISSION: Contact site.
ACCESSIBILITY: Contact site.
DESCRIPTION: The Selinsky-Green Farmhouse Museum represents the history of a typical family of the late nineteenth century. The log salt-box farmhouse, built by Prussian immigrants John and Mary Selinsky, was moved and restored by volunteers and now houses changing exhibits, period-decorated rooms, and special events. The farmhouse is located behind the St. Clair Shores Public Library.
URL: *www.scslibrary.org/sgfm.html*
CONTACT: parrk@libcoop.net • (586) 771-9020

STERLING HEIGHTS

William Upton House

ADDRESS: 40433 Utica Rd., Sterling Heights, MI 48313
ADMISSION: Contact site.
ACCESSIBILITY: Partially accessible.
DESCRIPTION: The William Upton House features household accessories, personal artifacts, maps, photographs, and documents relating to personal, business, educational, cultural, and recreational activities. The Sterling Heights Historical Commission solicits and accepts items that depict growth and change within the municipality from inception as a township in 1835 to the present.
URL: *www.sterling-heights.net/506/Historical-Commission*
CONTACT: turgeont@libcoop.net • (586) 446-2495

TAYLOR

Coan Lake Historical Walk at Heritage Park

ADDRESS: 12111 Pardee Rd., Taylor, MI 48180
ADMISSION: Free. Donations accepted.
ACCESSIBILITY: Fully accessible.
DESCRIPTION: Visit Taylor's Coan Lake Historical Walk at Heritage Park. Structures include the Taylor Historical Museum, a log cabin, a township hall, a church, a one-room schoolhouse, a mill with waterwheel, and farmhouses dating to late 1800s and early 1900s. The city's transportation past can also be explored via the society's replica train station, Fitz caboose, and Pere Marquette boxcar.
URL: *www.taylormichiganhistoricalsociety.org*
CONTACT: taylorhistoricalsociety@gmail.com • (313) 383-9271

TECUMSEH

Tecumseh Historical Museum

ADDRESS: 302 E Chicago Blvd., Tecumseh, MI 49286
ADMISSION: Free. Donations accepted.
ACCESSIBILITY: Contact site.
DESCRIPTION: The museum is housed in a 1913 fieldstone church that served as the first Catholic mission church in Tecumseh. Inside are many displays of the business and industry sites in the area, as well as information about Native-American history; the Perry Hayden Tithing Project and Henry Ford's involvement; and the agricultural history of celery and egg farms.
URL: *www.historictecumseh.org*
CONTACT: historictecumseh@gmail.com • (517) 423-2374

TROY

Troy Historic Village

ADDRESS: 60 W. Wattles Rd., Troy, MI 48089
ADMISSION: Charge.
ACCESSIBILITY: Fully accessible.
DESCRIPTION: Troy Historic Village showcases ten historic structures on a five-acre complex. Visitors can explore Michigan history by witnessing and sharing the lifestyles of the pioneers who established homes and farms in rural Troy Township during the 1800s. The village aims to enhance appreciation of history while using Troy's rich and evolving story as a backdrop.
URL: *www.troyhistoricvillage.org*
CONTACT: info@thvmail.org • (248) 524-3570

VASSAR

Vassar Historical Society Museum

ADDRESS: 450 S. Main St., Vassar, MI 48768
ADMISSION: Free. Donations accepted.
ACCESSIBILITY: Fully accessible.
DESCRIPTION: The Vassar Historical Society promotes an interest in the history of Vassar and the surrounding area. The museum—which is housed in a local historical home—features exhibits that change annually, as well as displays on area pioneer Townsend North, lumbering, schools, and the local opera house.
URL: *www.vassarhistory.org*
CONTACT: Contact via website. • (989) 823-2651

Watrousville Museum

ADDRESS: 4607 W. Caro Rd., Vassar, MI 48768
ADMISSION: Free. Donations accepted.
ACCESSIBILITY: Contact site.
DESCRIPTION: The Watrousville-Caro Area Historical Society is located within the former Watrousville General Store. The museum showcases artifacts from the 1850s from a typical rural Michigan lumber town. Installed to entice Abraham Lincoln to run for a second term, the "Lincoln Flagpole" on the museum lawn is the last known one still standing.
URL: *Facebook: Watrousville - Caro Area Historical Society*
CONTACT: (989) 551-6361

WARREN

Warren Historical Gallery

ADDRESS: 5460 Arden, Warren, MI 48092
ADMISSION: Contact site.
ACCESSIBILITY: Fully accessible.
DESCRIPTION: The historical gallery, located within the Warren Community Center, shows a visual history of the city of Warren from the swamp to the present. Some of the special collections include a flat iron collection, Warren High School class composites, a genealogy display, woodworking tools, and artifacts of Warren businesses. Guided tours are available for groups by appointment.
URL: *www.cityofwarren.org/index.php/historical-commission*
CONTACT: histcomm@cityofwarren.org • (586) 258-2056

WASHINGTON

Greater Washington Area Historical Society Museum

ADDRESS: 58230 Van Dyke, Washington, MI 48094
ADMISSION: Free. Donations accepted.
ACCESSIBILITY: Contact site.
DESCRIPTION: The museum features an extensive display on George Washington, which includes many pictures and commemorative items from the country's bicentennial. The war room has items from the Civil War, World War I, World War II, and Desert Storm. Many models of army vehicles are on display. A Boy Scout Museum is also housed inside the museum.
URL: *www.washhistsoc.org*
CONTACT: holcomi@comcast.net • (586) 786-5304

Loren Andrus Octagon House

ADDRESS: 57500 Van Dyke, Washington, MI 48094
ADMISSION: Charge.
ACCESSIBILITY: Partially accessible.
DESCRIPTION: Step back in time and enjoy the history of the Washington community at the Loren Andrus Octagon House. Built in 1860, the house has served the area as a farm, restaurant, school, and museum throughout its history. Today, the house's furnishings include items spanning all those periods.
URL: *www.octagonhouse.org*
CONTACT: info@octagonhouse.org • (586) 781-0084

WATERFORD

Waterford Township Historic Village

ADDRESS: 4490 Hatchery Rd., Waterford, MI 48329
ADMISSION: Free. Donations accepted.
ACCESSIBILITY: Partially accessible.
DESCRIPTION: Waterford Township Historical Society's Historic Village sits on the banks of the Clinton River in Fish Hatchery Park. Some of the buildings are original, while others are either exact replicas or representations of what they would have looked like in the early 1900s. Hands-on activities are available for kids and adults. Booklets and audio boxes make self-guided tours easy.
URL: *www.waterfordhistoricalsociety.org*
CONTACT: sstrait649@comcast.net • (248) 683-2697

WAYNE

Wayne Historical Museum

ADDRESS: 1 Towne Square St., Wayne, MI 48184
ADMISSION: Free. Donations accepted.
ACCESSIBILITY: Fully accessible.
DESCRIPTION: View a collection of old photographs and family histories or explore carriages from the Prouty and Glass Carriage Works during your visit to the Wayne Historical Museum. Artifacts on display come from local businesses, theaters, farms, first-responder departments, and a collection of graduation class pictures from the late 1880s through the 1980s.
URL: *www.waynehistoricalmuseum.wordpress.com*
CONTACT: waynehistoricalsociety@gmail.com • (734) 722-0113

WESTLAND

Westland Historic Village

ADDRESS: 857 N. Wayne Rd., Westland, MI 48185
ADMISSION: Free. Donations accepted.
ACCESSIBILITY: Partially accessible.
DESCRIPTION: The Westland Historic Village is a collection of buildings including a farmhouse built before the Civil War—with artifacts from 1850 to 1899—and an octagon house also built before the Civil War which contains artifacts from 1900 to the 1950s. There is also a building that houses the Eloise Hospital Museum exhibit, which was the local poorhouse and asylum.
URL: *www.whvp66.weebly.com*
CONTACT: whvp66@gmail.com • (734) 477-5343

WHITE LAKE

Kelley-Fisk Farm

ADDRESS: 9180 Highland Rd., White Lake, MI 48383
ADMISSION: Contact site.
ACCESSIBILITY: Fully accessible.
DESCRIPTION: The Kelley-Fisk Farm features an 1855 farmhouse completely furnished with antiques and surrounded by outbuildings including corn cribs, garage, and pig and hen houses. The site also includes an 1876 one-room school, turn-of-the-century barn full of farm related antiques, and a 1930s kitchen display.
URL: *www.whitelakehistory.org*
CONTACT: whitelakehistoricalsociety@gmail.com • (248) 698-3300

WIXOM

Wixom-Wire House Museum

ADDRESS: 687 North Wixom Rd., Wixom, MI 48393
ADMISSION: Contact site.
ACCESSIBILITY: Contact site.
DESCRIPTION: The Wixom-Wire House was originally built in 1855 as a parsonage. In addition to being a residence, the house was used for worship and funeral services until the permanent church was built in 1865. The Gothic Revival style home features period furnishings, a parlor alcove which originally held coffins, a 1920s kitchen with a hand pump, and an original outhouse.
URL: *www.wixomhistoricalsociety.org*
CONTACT: laure.dorchak@wixomhistoricalsociety.org • (248) 624-3950

WYANDOTTE

Ford-MacNichol Home

ADDRESS: 2610 Biddle Ave., Wyandotte, MI 48192
ADMISSION: Contact site.
ACCESSIBILITY: Contact site.
DESCRIPTION: The 1896 Ford-MacNichol Home is the main exhibit building of the Wyandotte Museums' campus and houses the majority of the artifact collection. In this historic house setting, a vivid picture of early-twentieth-century Wyandotte is recreated with elegantly appointed rooms and rotating exhibits on local history.
URL: *www.wyandottehistory.org*
CONTACT: wyandottehistory@gmail.com • (734) 324-7284

Marx Home

ADDRESS: 2630 Biddle Ave., Wyandotte, MI 48192
ADMISSION: Contact site.
ACCESSIBILITY: Contact site.
DESCRIPTION: The historic Marx Home, built in 1862, is a beautiful example of an Italianate-style townhome, featuring a red-brick exterior, ornamental ironwork, double entrance door, and hooded windows. The home is now used as a community space wherein groups can gather on the first floor for presentations, gatherings, lectures, and meetings.
URL: *www.wyandottehistory.org*
CONTACT: wyandottehistory@gmail.com • (734) 324-7284

YPSILANTI

Michigan Firehouse Museum

ADDRESS: 110 W. Cross St., Ypsilanti, MI 48197
ADMISSION: Charge.
ACCESSIBILITY: Fully accessible.
DESCRIPTION: The museum preserves firefighting history and promotes fire safety. Comprised of an original 1898 firehouse with a restored bunk area and a 12,000-square-foot exhibit space on three levels, the museum displays more than 27 fire rigs as well as bells, lights, sirens, helmets, extinguishers, alarms, and other fire-related equipment.
URL: *www.michiganfirehousemuseum.org*
CONTACT: info@michiganfirehousemuseum.org • (734) 547-0663

Ypsilanti Auto Heritage Museum

ADDRESS: 100 E. Cross St., Ypsilanti, MI 48198
ADMISSION: Charge.
ACCESSIBILITY: Fully accessible.
DESCRIPTION: The museum preserves an important era in Michigan history when Ypsilanti served as a thriving commercial and manufacturing hub. Displays include Motor State which held patents on power convertible tops, the Ford Motor Company Generator Plant, and local car dealerships.
URL: *www.ypsiautoheritage.org*
CONTACT: info@ypsiautoheritage.org • (734) 482-5200

Ypsilanti Historical Society Museum

ADDRESS: 220 N. Huron St., Ypsilanti, MI 48197
ADMISSION: Free. Donations accepted.
ACCESSIBILITY: Partially accessible.
DESCRIPTION: The Ypsilanti Historical Society Museum is a house museum set in an 1860 Italianate home. Nineteenth- and twentieth-century artifacts are displayed as well as exhibits depicting Ypsilanti's heritage. The Ypsilanti Historical Society Archives is located in the lower level of the museum and is open to the public interested in researching Ypsilanti's history.
URL: *www.ypsilantihistoricalsociety.org*
CONTACT: yhs.museum@gmail.com • (734) 217-8236

EASTERN

NORTHERN REGION

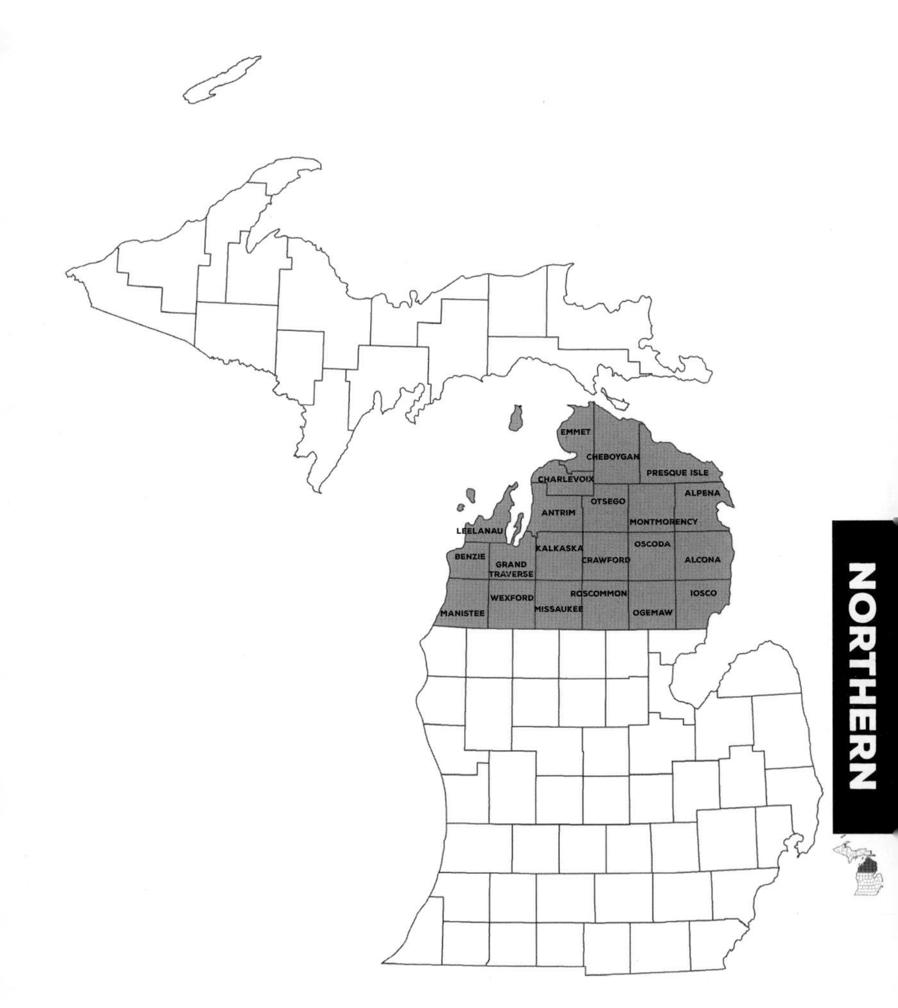

ALDEN

Alden Depot Museum

ADDRESS: 10670 Coy St., Alden, MI 49612
ADMISSION: Free. Donations accepted.
ACCESSIBILITY: Fully accessible.
DESCRIPTION: The restored 1907 Pere Marquette Depot and Park beckons! Young and old delight in the extensive permanent collection of working model railroad layouts. Outside, climb aboard the vintage engine, boxcar, and caboose. Exhibits and collections include books, postcards, photographs, documents, and artifacts which showcase early industry and resort life.
URL: *www.aldendepot.com*
CONTACT: aldendepot@gmail.com • No phone listed.

ALPENA

Besser Museum for Northeast Michigan

ADDRESS: 491 Johnson St., Alpena, MI 49707
ADMISSION: Contact site.
ACCESSIBILITY: Fully accessible.
DESCRIPTION: The Besser Museum for Northeast Michigan provides the public with enriching cultural experiences in art, history, and science. The museum houses a full dome planetarium and a two-story Foucault pendulum and offers the opportunity to dig and keep the fossils found in the outdoor Lafarge Fossil Park exhibit. Art exhibits rotate through an extensive collection of fine art.
URL: *www.bessermuseum.org*
CONTACT: bessermuseum@bessermuseum.org • (989) 356-2202

Great Lakes Maritime Heritage Center

ADDRESS: 500 West Fletcher St., Alpena, MI 49707
ADMISSION: Free. Donations accepted.
ACCESSIBILITY: Fully accessible.
DESCRIPTION: Explore the visitors center to the Thunder Bay National Marine Sanctuary. Visitors will learn how the sanctuary studies lake floor resources, and works to safeguard the Great Lakes and their rich maritime history. Glass-bottom boat tours are also available. The site is part of the Michigan History Center's Museum System.
URL: *www.thunderbay.noaa.gov*
CONTACT: thunderbay@noaa.gov • (989) 884-6200

Thunder Bay National Marine Sanctuary

ADDRESS: 500 W. Fletcher St., Alpena, MI 49707
ADMISSION: Contact site.
ACCESSIBILITY: Contact site.
DESCRIPTION: Managed jointly by the Thunder Bay National Marine Sanctuary and the Alpena County George M. Fletcher Public Library, the research collection is dedicated to Great Lakes maritime history. The strength of the collection is nineteenth-century Great Lakes shipbuilding technology, but it also includes information about other maritime history topics.
URL: *www.thunderbay.noaa.gov*
CONTACT: thunderbay@noaa.gov • (989) 884-6200

ARCADIA

Arcadia Area Historical Museum

ADDRESS: 3340 Lake St., Arcadia, MI 49613
ADMISSION: Contact site.
ACCESSIBILITY: Fully accessible.
DESCRIPTION: The Arcadia Area Historical Society manages the museum in an 1884 Victorian house built by an early settler named Howard Gilbert. The museum contains artifacts that pertain to lumbering in Arcadia, furniture from the Arcadia Furniture Co., shipping, local businesses, and Harriet Quimby.

URL: *www.arcadiami.com*
CONTACT: lmatt613@msn.com • (231) 970-0528

BEAVER ISLAND

Heritage Park

ADDRESS: 26400 Donegal Bay Rd., Beaver Island, MI 49782
ADMISSION: Free. Donations accepted.
ACCESSIBILITY: Contact site.
DESCRIPTION: Items available to view at Heritage Park include the Island's last thresher, the generator that first provided power, an old tilt-wheel grader, and a barn. Each is on a slab and under a free-standing roof. The site is run by the Beaver Island Historical Society.

URL: *www.beaverislandhistory.org*
CONTACT: bihistory@tds.net • (231) 448-2254

Marine Museum

ADDRESS: 26275 Main St., Beaver Island, MI 49782
ADMISSION: Free. Donations accepted.
ACCESSIBILITY: Contact site.
DESCRIPTION: The Marine Museum includes exhibits and materials about shipbuilding, various vessels, diving activities, and information about the other islands in the Beaver Archipelago. Visitors can also learn about maritime disasters in the area and efforts by the Coast Guard and Lighthouse Services. The site is run by the Beaver Island Historical Society.

URL: *www.beaverislandhistory.org*
CONTACT: bihistory@tds.net • (231) 448-2254

Mormon Print Shop Museum

ADDRESS: 26275 Main St., Beaver Island, MI 49782
ADMISSION: Free. Donations accepted.
ACCESSIBILITY: Fully accessible.
DESCRIPTION: The Print Shop serves as the general museum for the Beaver Island Historical Society. Housed in the print shop that was built by the followers of James Jesse Strang in 1850, it includes displays about Strang and his times, early Irish life, Native-American inhabitants, musicians, and more. The site is run by the Beaver Island Historical Society.

URL: *www.beaverislandhistory.org*
CONTACT: bihistory@tds.net • (231) 448-2254

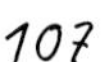

Protar's Home

ADDRESS: Sloptown Rd., Beaver Island, MI 49782
ADMISSION: Free. Donations accepted.
ACCESSIBILITY: Contact site.
DESCRIPTION: Visitors can explore an early Irish built log cabin, which is furnished with Protar's furniture. Protar was a beloved man on Beaver Island who was regarded as the island doctor during the late 1800s and early 1900s. The site is run by the Beaver Island Historical Society.

URL: *www.beaverislandhistory.org*
CONTACT: bihistory@tds.net • (231) 448-2254

BELLAIRE

Bellaire Area Museum

ADDRESS: 202 N. Bridge St., Bellaire, MI 49615
ADMISSION: Free. Donations accepted.
ACCESSIBILITY: Fully accessible.
DESCRIPTION: The Bellaire Area Historical Society informs and educates the residents of, and visitors to, Bellaire of its history. The Bellaire Historical Museum features Civil War uniforms and weapons, a pioneer cabin, the history of Bellaire High School, and the story of largest woodenware factory in the world.

URL: *Facebook: Bellaire Area Historical Society*
CONTACT: bellairehistoricalsociety@gmail.com • (231) 533-8254

BENZONIA

Benzie Area Historical Museum

ADDRESS: 6941 Traverse Ave., Benzonia, MI 49616
ADMISSION: Free. Donations accepted.
ACCESSIBILITY: Fully accessible.
DESCRIPTION: Visit the Benzie Area Historical Museum to view exhibits representing changes from early logging and agriculture to the establishment of a religious community, the railroads and advent of the car ferries, fruit orchards, and now tourism. The museum, housed in an 1886 Congregational Church, is on the Michigan State Register of Historic Sites.

URL: *www.benziemuseum.org*
CONTACT: info@benziemuseum.org • (231) 882-5539

BRETHREN

Brethren Heritage Association Museum

ADDRESS: 14300 Cart Ave., Brethren, MI 49619
ADMISSION: Free. Donations accepted.
ACCESSIBILITY: Fully accessible.
DESCRIPTION: Four buildings on the site include a reconstructed, authentic cabin from the 1940s; a reconstructed store from the 1930s; and a tool shed containing many artifacts from the lumbering era. The Brethren Heritage Association's collections contain items related to homesteading, area churches, logging, and farming. Early family records are also available to researchers.

URL: *Facebook: Brethren Heritage Association*
CONTACT: janetdonstroup@gmail.com • (231) 477-5526

CENTRAL LAKE

Knowles Historical Museum

ADDRESS: 2238 Main St., Central Lake, MI 49622
ADMISSION: Contact site.
ACCESSIBILITY: Contact site.
DESCRIPTION: The Central Lake Area Historical Society maintains the Knowles Historical Museum in a restored home that is furnished with local period furniture, including a 1904 pump organ. The museum also offers a 100-year collection of a local newspaper, *The Central Lake Torch*, as well as many tapes, pictures, books by local authors, and genealogy research materials.
URL: *Facebook: Central Lake Area Historical Society*
CONTACT: (231) 544-6314

CHARLEVOIX

Castle Farms

ADDRESS: 5052 M-66, Charlevoix, MI 49720
ADMISSION: Charge.
ACCESSIBILITY: Fully accessible.
DESCRIPTION: Journey to the beautiful castle and gardens, discover the story of this historic property built in 1918, and learn fascinating details about its restoration. Interact with the largest model railroad in Michigan, enjoy the extensive gardens and reflection pond, and view the dragon. Visit the museum that has collections of 1918 memorabilia, antique toys, and World War I artifacts.
URL: *www.castlefarms.com*
CONTACT: info@castlefarms.com • (231) 237-0884

Charlevoix Railroad Depot

ADDRESS: 305 Chicago Ave., Charlevoix, MI 49720
ADMISSION: Contact site.
ACCESSIBILITY: Fully accessible.
DESCRIPTION: Built by the Chicago & West Michigan Railway in 1892, the depot is used for meetings, events, and occasional exhibits. The depot is listed on the National Register of Historic Places and the interior may be viewed upon request. On the exterior, the Charlevoix Area Garden Club has developed an award-winning heritage garden that is always open to the public.
URL: *www.chxhistory.com*
CONTACT: info@chxhistory.com • (231) 547-0373

Charlevoix South Pier Lighthouse

ADDRESS: Lake Michigan Municipal Beach, Charlevoix, MI 49720
ADMISSION: Contact site.
ACCESSIBILITY: Partially accessible.
DESCRIPTION: The Charlevoix Historical Society is responsible for the preservation, restoration, and maintenance of the Charlevoix South Pier Lighthouse. The federal government owns the pier, the city of Charlevoix owns the light, and the Coast Guard maintains the light as an aid to navigation. The black lens housing at the top is from the original Charlevoix light that was built in 1885.
URL: *www.chxhistory.com*
CONTACT: info@chxhistory.com • (231) 547-0373

Harsha House

ADDRESS: 103 State St., Charlevoix, MI 49720
ADMISSION: Contact site.
ACCESSIBILITY: Contact site.
DESCRIPTION: The museum includes three restored 1891 Victorian parlors with vintage furnishings and original works of art by Charlevoix artists. It has kitchen and household objects on display. Other attractions include a large one-horse open sleigh, rotating exhibits, a pedal pump reed organ, a working wind-up Victrola, and 3 1/2-order Fresnel lens from the Gray's Reef Lighthouse.
URL: *www.chxhistory.com*
CONTACT: info@chxhistory.com • (231) 547-0373

Norwood Historic Schoolhouse

ADDRESS: 742 4th St., Charlevoix, MI 49720
ADMISSION: Contact site.
ACCESSIBILITY: Contact site.
DESCRIPTION: Collections housed in the preserved 1890 schoolhouse include documents and photos relating to nineteenth-century settlement and lumbering, local schools, and famous personages. Also included are some oral history transcripts and tapes. During the summer, the Norwood Area Historical Society hosts educational events and social gatherings.
URL: *Facebook: Norwood Area Historical Society*
CONTACT: nahsschoolhouse@gmail.com • (231) 547-6220

CHEBOYGAN

Cheboygan River Front Range Lighthouse

ADDRESS: 606 Water St., Cheboygan, MI 49721
ADMISSION: Contact site.
ACCESSIBILITY: Contact site.
DESCRIPTION: The Great Lakes Lighthouse Keepers Association obtained the Cheboygan River Front Range Lighthouse in 2004 under the National Historic Lighthouse Preservation Act. The lighthouse is currently being restored to its circa 1910 appearance, a time when Cheboygan lumber mills were shipping a large amount of products throughout the Great Lakes.
URL: *www.gllka.org*
CONTACT: info@gllka.com • (231) 436-5580

COPEMISH

Marilla Museum & Pioneer Place

ADDRESS: 9991 Marilla Rd., Copemish, MI 49625
ADMISSION: Free. Donations accepted.
ACCESSIBILITY: Partially accessible.
DESCRIPTION: The Marilla Museum & Pioneer Place contains a restored two-story 1870s Pioneer House, a large 1900s barn, and a full-size replica hunter-trapper's cabin. Each home is fully furnished and reflects early rural pioneer living. The barn includes many farm machines and implements, with displays representing Marilla's rich logging history. Teas and tours are available by special arrangement.
URL: *www.marillahistory.org*
CONTACT: marillamuseum@gmail.com • (231) 383-1630

EAST JORDAN

East Jordan City Hall

ADDRESS: 201 Main St., East Jordan, MI 49727
ADMISSION: Free. Donations accepted.
ACCESSIBILITY: Contact site.
DESCRIPTION: Collections include furnishings, train memorabilia, woodworking tools, and revolving displays. Exhibits include information on local historian George Secord, memorabilia from the Hite and Gidley Drug Stores, a game display, and women's fashions and accessories from bygone eras. Exhibits are updated annually, so each visit is a new experience.
URL: *www.portsideartsfair.org*
CONTACT: portsideartsfair@gmail.com • (231) 675-4841

East Jordan Portside Art & Historical Society Museum

ADDRESS: 1656 S M 66, East Jordan, MI 49727
ADMISSION: Free. Donations accepted.
ACCESSIBILITY: Fully accessible.
DESCRIPTION: The East Jordan Portside Art & Historical Society Museum is located in Elm Pointe Park, a Michigan historic site located on Lake Charlevoix. It was established in 1976 to preserve the history of the local area. Collections include the lumbering era, trains, agriculture, home life, military, and industries.
URL: *www.portsideartsfair.org*
CONTACT: portsideartsfair@gmail.com • (231) 675-4841

Raven Hill Discovery Center

ADDRESS: 4737 Fuller Rd., East Jordan, MI 49727
ADMISSION: Charge.
ACCESSIBILITY: Fully accessible.
DESCRIPTION: The Raven Hill Discovery Center provides opportunities for all ages to learn, create, grow, and play through classes, exhibits, and facilities. The center creates meaningful learning connections by linking history, science, and the arts. The site serves as a regional science and technology center, as well as a cultural, historical, and art center.
URL: *www.miravenhill.org*
CONTACT: info@miravenhill.org • (231) 536-3369

EAST TAWAS

Iosco County Historical Society & Museum

ADDRESS: 405 W. Bay St., East Tawas, MI 48730
ADMISSION: Contact site.
ACCESSIBILITY: Fully accessible.
DESCRIPTION: In 1978, the society opened its museum as a depository of historical artifacts reflecting Iosco County's history and growth. Historical displays and exhibits change regularly and include class pictures; a Victorian parlor; an early kitchen; medical displays; a Western States ship; and the military during World War I, World War II, and the Spanish American and Civil Wars.
URL: *Facebook: Iosco County Historical Society*
CONTACT: iosco.history@gmail.com • (989) 362-8911

Tawas Point Lighthouse

ADDRESS: 686 Tawas Beach Rd., East Tawas, MI 48730
ADMISSION: Recreation Passport required.
ACCESSIBILITY: Contact site.
DESCRIPTION: In operation from 1876 to 2016, the Tawas Point Lighthouse was built to guide vessels safely into Tawas Bay. Visitor tours interpret life at the lighthouse and the area's maritime history. The point is a mecca for birders—especially during the migration seasons of spring and fall. The site is part of the Michigan History Center's Museum System.
URL: *www.michigan.gov/tawaslighthouse*
CONTACT: mhcinfo@michigan.gov • (517) 930-3806

ELK RAPIDS

Elk Rapids Area Historical Society Museum

ADDRESS: 301 Traverse St., Elk Rapids, MI 49629
ADMISSION: Charge.
ACCESSIBILITY: Fully accessible.
DESCRIPTION: Displays focus on the Elk Rapids area and its role in the "Chain of Lakes" during the nineteenth and twentieth centuries. Collections include artifacts from the lumbering, cement, and pig-iron industries as well as vintage clothing, tools, and antique furniture. The building is listed on the National Register of Historic Places and the Michigan State Register of Historic Sites.
URL: *www.elkrapidshistory.org*
CONTACT: president@elkrapidshistory.org • (231) 264-5692

EMPIRE

Empire Area Museum Complex

ADDRESS: 11544 So. LaCore Rd., Empire, MI 49630
ADMISSION: Free. Donations accepted.
ACCESSIBILITY: Fully accessible.
DESCRIPTION: The Empire Area Museum complex includes four buildings featuring a turn-of-the-century saloon, a sail and rail display, a 1924 vintage gas station, horse-drawn vehicles, and a "hit and miss" engine display. The museum also includes a one-room school, a 1911 "hose house" firehouse, a set of "Big Wheels" for logging, and farming and lumbering equipment.
URL: *www.empiremimuseum.org*
CONTACT: empiremuseum@yahoo.com • (231) 326-5568

FIFE LAKE

Fife Lake Area Historical Museum

ADDRESS: 136 W State St., Fife Lake, MI 49633
ADMISSION: Free. Donations accepted.
ACCESSIBILITY: Fully accessible.
DESCRIPTION: The Fife Lake Area Historical Museum has items dating back to the era before European settlers arrived in the region. Visitors can view Native-American artifacts, a variety of working antiques, historical clothing, a general store, and displays on logging and railroading in the area. There is also a large collage mural of pictures from the 1800s.
URL: *www.fifelakehistoricalsociety.org*
CONTACT: fifelakehistoricalsociety@gmail.com • (989) 781-0512

Fife Lake Fire Barn

ADDRESS: 117 W State St., Fife Lake, MI 49633
ADMISSION: Free. Donations accepted.
ACCESSIBILITY: Fully accessible.
DESCRIPTION: Originally constructed in 1876 as a school, this structure is believed to be one of the community's oldest surviving buildings. Now, the fire barn houses medical and firefighting information and artifacts—including uniforms from 120 years ago. A 1937 Chevrolet fire truck and a doctor's sleigh are among the many points of interest.
URL: *www.fifelakehistoricalsociety.org*
CONTACT: fifelakehistoricalsociety@gmail.com • (989) 781-0512

Fife Lake Historical School House

ADDRESS: 137 W State St., Fife Lake, MI 49633
ADMISSION: Free. Donations accepted.
ACCESSIBILITY: Fully accessible.
DESCRIPTION: The 1878 schoolhouse—the first school in lower Fife Lake—houses a realistic representation of a nineteenth-century, one-room schoolhouse. It has carved desks, McGuffey Eclectic Readers, a potbelly stove, and an American flag from the 1870s. Rules for teachers and students of that era are listed inside. A separate room houses the genealogy library of many Fife Lake families.
URL: *www.fifelakehistoricalsociety.org*
CONTACT: fifelakehistoricalsociety@gmail.com • (989) 781-0512

FRANKFORT

Point Betsie Lighthouse

ADDRESS: 3701 Point Betsie Rd., Frankfort, MI 49635
ADMISSION: Charge.
ACCESSIBILITY: Fully accessible.
DESCRIPTION: All of the historic buildings operated by the Friends of Point Betsie Lighthouse, Inc., have been completely restored, including the inside of the lighthouse and fog signal building. The Boathouse Museum includes a U.S. Coast Guard rescue boat and other tools used by lifesavers. Don't miss the gift shop and consider renting the Assistant Keeper's Apartment.
URL: *www.pointbetsie.org*
CONTACT: info@pointbetsie.org • (231) 352-7644

GRAYLING

Crawford County Historical Society Museum

ADDRESS: 97 East Michigan Ave., Grayling, MI 49738
ADMISSION: Free. Donations accepted.
ACCESSIBILITY: Partially accessible.
DESCRIPTION: The Crawford County Historical Society maintains a museum complex that includes an 1882 historic train depot, a 1900 schoolhouse that is used to exhibit the military history of Crawford County, a log trapper's cabin, a firehouse with two restored fire engines, a farm building with a restored tractor, an early 1900 cutter sleigh, and a retired 1920s caboose.
URL: *www.crawfordcountyhistoricalsociety.com*
CONTACT: cchsgrayling@gmail.com • (989) 745-3493

Hartwick Pines Logging Museum

ADDRESS: 3612 State Park Dr., Grayling, MI 49738
ADMISSION: Recreation Passport required.
ACCESSIBILITY: Fully accessible.
DESCRIPTION: The Hartwick Pines Logging Museum returns visitors to the state's nineteenth-century logging era, when Michigan led the nation in sawed lumber production. Indoor and outdoor exhibits, period rooms, and live interpreters tell the stories of loggers, river men, and entrepreneurs. The site is part of the Michigan History Center's Museum System.
URL: *www.michigan.gov/loggingmuseum*
CONTACT: mhcinfo@michigan.gov • (989) 348-2537

Wellington Farm Park

ADDRESS: 6944 S. Military Rd., Grayling, MI 49738
ADMISSION: Charge.
ACCESSIBILITY: Partially accessible.
DESCRIPTION: Over 15 fully functional buildings and sites present insight into family and farm life during the Great Depression. There is a working sawmill, a working gristmill, and a livestock barn. Along with numerous pieces of farm machinery, there are two operating steam traction engines. The Perry Lamkin displays one of a kind artifacts utilized in the manufacture of wooden handles.
URL: *www.wellingtonfarmusa.com*
CONTACT: Contact via website. • (989) 348-5187

HARBOR SPRINGS

Harbor Springs History Museum

ADDRESS: 349 East Main St., Harbor Springs, MI 49740
ADMISSION: Free. Donations accepted.
ACCESSIBILITY: Fully accessible.
DESCRIPTION: Located in the former city hall building on Main Street, the Harbor Springs History Museum documents the unique history of the area. The exhibits escort visitors through time, from the area's first residents—the Odawa—to the missionaries, homesteaders, loggers, merchants, and resorters who later lived there.
URL: *www.harborspringshistory.org*
CONTACT: info@harborspringshistory.org • (231) 526-9771

HARRISVILLE

Sturgeon Point Lighthouse and Old Bailey School

ADDRESS: 6071 Point Rd., Harrisville, MI 48470
ADMISSION: Free. Donations accepted.
ACCESSIBILITY: Partially accessible.
DESCRIPTION: Visitors can experience educational tours and programs at the Sturgeon Point Lighthouse and Bailey School. The Sturgeon Point Lighthouse features an authentic lens, keeper's home, and two boats used by the Coast Guard. Also on site is the actual Alcona County one-room schoolhouse, completely restored and furnished with authentic collections.
URL: *www.alconahistoricalsociety.com*
CONTACT: ahs@alconahistoricalsociety.com • (989) 471-2088

HILLMAN

Brush Creek Mill

ADDRESS: 121 State St., Hillman, MI 49746
ADMISSION: Contact site.
ACCESSIBILITY: Fully accessible.
DESCRIPTION: The Hillman Area Historical and Genealogy Society runs the museum on the second floor of the Bush Creek Mill. Displays feature artifacts that represent the history of the area and building tours and demonstrations of the grist mill operations are available by appointment. There is also a memorial garden and gift shop that features art and crafts by local artists.
URL: *www.brushcreekmill.org*
CONTACT: brushcreekmill@gmail.com • (989) 742-2527

HONOR

Drake School Museum

ADDRESS: Corner of Fowler and Valley Roads, Honor, MI 49640
ADMISSION: Free. Donations accepted.
ACCESSIBILITY: Contact site.
DESCRIPTION: Visit the Drake School Museum and experience what it was like to be a student in the early twentieth century. The Drake School was built in 1891 and used as a school until 1943 at its present location. An agriculture exhibit shares the stories of the local farm families and tours are also available by appointment.
URL: *www.benziemuseum.org*
CONTACT: info@benziemuseum.org • (231) 882-5539

KALEVA

Bottle House Museum

ADDRESS: 14551 Wuoksi St., Kaleva, MI 49645
ADMISSION: Contact site.
ACCESSIBILITY: Contact site.
DESCRIPTION: The Bottle House was constructed by John Makinen, who used 60,000 chipped or flawed bottles from his local pop bottling factory. He even incorporated different colored bottles to create artistic designs and words within the walls of his house. Inside the museum, exhibits relate to the early settlement of Kaleva, Finnish-American culture, and early-twentieth-century farm life.
URL: *www.kalevamichigan.com/bottle-house-museum*
CONTACT: caasiala@jackpine.com • (231) 362-2080

LAKE ANN

Almira Historical Society Museum

ADDRESS: 19440 Maple St., Lake Ann, MI 49650
ADMISSION: Contact site.
ACCESSIBILITY: Fully accessible.
DESCRIPTION: The museum has more than 1,300 artifacts and includes the Thompson-Kuemin House. The property also includes the Almira Fire Barn Museum, which houses a 1946 international fire truck, a blacksmith shop, and boathouse. Exhibits include military uniforms and American flags, vintage switchboards, early logging and farming equipment, and a fire display.
URL: *www.almiramuseum.org*
CONTACT: almirahist@gmail.com • (231) 275-5847

Fishtown

ADDRESS: 201 W. River St., Leland, MI 49654
ADMISSION: Free. Donations accepted.
ACCESSIBILITY: Fully accessible.
DESCRIPTION: Fishtown is a collection of fishing shanties, smokehouses, overhanging docks, fish tugs and charter boats along the Leland River. Fishtown attractions include a Welcome Center with exhibits about Fishtown's past and present as a working waterfront, historic fishing shanties containing unique shops, an operating fishery, and active commercial fishing tugs *Joy* and *Janice Sue*.
URL: *www.fishtownmi.org*
CONTACT: info@fishtownmi.org • (231) 256-8878

Leelanau Historical Society Museum

ADDRESS: 203 East Cedar St., Leland, MI 49654
ADMISSION: Charge.
ACCESSIBILITY: Fully accessible.
DESCRIPTION: The Leelanau Historical Society is a museum, gift shop, and research center located on the banks of the Leland River, and two blocks away from historic Fishtown. Permanent and rotating exhibits include a variety of topics about the Leelanau Peninsula's past of logging, agriculture, early mapping, the Anishinaabek culture, Early European settlers, transportation, and lighthouses.
URL: *www.leelanauhistory.org*
CONTACT: info@leelanauhistory.org • (231) 256-7475

North Manitou Shoal Light Station

ADDRESS: Leland Harbor, 107 N. Lake St., Leland, MI 49654
ADMISSION: Charge.
ACCESSIBILITY: Contact site.
DESCRIPTION: North Manitou Light Keepers is a team of stewards dedicated to rehabilitating, maintaining, and appreciating the North Manitou Shoal Light Station in Leelanau County. This offshore lighthouse, known locally as "The Crib" due to its design, is a wonderful piece of Lake Michigan maritime history. Tours are available on the website.
URL: *www.northmanitoulightkeepers.org*
CONTACT: info@northmanitoulightkeepers.org • (517) 294-7859

Old Art Building

ADDRESS: 111 South Main St., Leland, MI 49654
ADMISSION: Free. Donations accepted.
ACCESSIBILITY: Fully accessible.
DESCRIPTION: The Old Art Building is a community center located in the heart of Leland, Michigan. The mission of the Leelanau Community Center non-profit is to promote the arts and cultural enrichment, provide a gathering place for the community, and preserve the Old Art Building for generations to come.
URL: *www.oldartbuilding.com*
CONTACT: info@oldartbuilding.com • (231) 256-2131

LEWISTON

Lewiston Area Museum

ADDRESS: 4384 Michelson Ave., Lewiston, MI 49756
ADMISSION: Contact site.
ACCESSIBILITY: Partially accessible.
DESCRIPTION: The museum is in the 1892 home of David Keenland, manager of the Michelson & Hanson Lumber Company. The home was later sold to the Sachs family, who occupied it for the next 85 years. The museum shares their histories and the histories of the families in the area. The site also features a fully furnished trapper's cabin and barn.
URL: *www.lewistonhistoricalsociety.com*
CONTACT: lewareahistsoc@gmail.com • (989) 786-2451

LINCOLN

Lincoln Train Depot

ADDRESS: Corner of Fiske and Lake Streets, Lincoln, MI 48742
ADMISSION: Free. Donations accepted.
ACCESSIBILITY: Partially accessible.
DESCRIPTION: The Lincoln Train Depot, a wood structure that has been standing since 1886, was built by the Detroit, Bay City, and Alpena Railroad. The depot is located on Lake Street in Lincoln and served the community and surrounding area until 1929. The display includes a caboose and switching engine.
URL: *www.alconahistoricalsociety.com*
CONTACT: ahs@alconahistoricalsociety.com • (989) 471-2088

LOVELLS

Lovells Township Historical Society Museum

ADDRESS: 8405 Twin Bridge Rd., Lovells, MI 49738
ADMISSION: Free. Donations accepted.
ACCESSIBILITY: Fully accessible.
DESCRIPTION: The society operates both the Lone Pine Schoolhouse Museum and the Lovells Museum of Trout Fishing History. The museum features period photos and gear as well as a permanent exhibit honoring conservationist and Trout Unlimited cofounder, Art Neumann. The historical society hosts a variety of programs and events throughout the year.
URL: *www.lthsmuseums.org*
CONTACT: lthsmuseums@gmail.com • (313) 320-6607

MACKINAW CITY

Colonial Michilimackinac

ADDRESS: 102 West Straits Ave., Mackinaw City, MI 49701
ADMISSION: Charge.
ACCESSIBILITY: Partially accessible.
DESCRIPTION: French fur-trading village and military outpost Michilimackinac was founded in 1715. Today, the site features a reconstructed, fortified village of 13 buildings as it appeared in the 1770s, based on evidence gathered during the nation's longest archaeological excavation.
URL: *www.mackinacparks.com*
CONTACT: mackinacparks@michigan.gov • (231) 436-4100

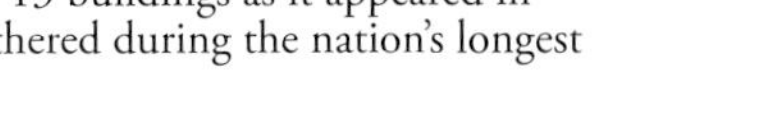

Historic Mill Creek Discovery Park

ADDRESS: 9001 US-23, Mackinaw City, MI 49701
ADMISSION: Charge.
ACCESSIBILITY: Partially accessible.
DESCRIPTION: The straits' first industrial complex, now the site of the Historic Mill Creek Discovery Park, provided lumber for the settlement of Mackinac Island in the 1790s. Attractions include demonstrations of hand-saw techniques and a reconstructed eighteenth-century water-driven sawmill. There are also natural history programs and daily "high ropes" adventure tours.
URL: *www.mackinacparks.com*
CONTACT: mackinacparks@michigan.gov • (231) 436-4100

Icebreaker Mackinaw Maritime Museum

ADDRESS: 707 North Huron Ave. #2, Mackinaw City, MI 49701
ADMISSION: Charge.
ACCESSIBILITY: Contact site.
DESCRIPTION: The United States Coast Guard Icebreaker *Mackinaw*, WAGB-83 is known as the "Queen of the Great Lakes" and the largest icebreaker on the Great Lakes. Decommissioned in 2006, she now resides at Mackinaw City and is open for public tours, educational tours, overnight encampments, and group events.
URL: *www.themackinaw.org*
CONTACT: officemanager@themackinaw.org • (231) 436-9825

Mackinaw Area Historical Society Heritage Village

ADDRESS: 1425 West Central Ave., Mackinaw City, MI 49701
ADMISSION: Free. Donations accepted.
ACCESSIBILITY: Partially accessible.
DESCRIPTION: The village includes a pestilence house, a church, the sawmill that cut the timbers for the Soo Locks, a one-room schoolhouse, a log cabin, the Stimpson Homestead, a machine shed, a tar-paper shack, wigwams, and more. Visitors can experience the history of the Straits area through hands-on activities and experiences for all ages.
URL: *www.mackinawhistory.org*
CONTACT: mackinawareahistoricalsociety@gmail.com • (812) 797-6000

Old Mackinac Point Lighthouse

ADDRESS: 526 North Huron Ave., Mackinaw City, MI 49701
ADMISSION: Charge.
ACCESSIBILITY: Partially accessible.
DESCRIPTION: A true gem of the Great Lakes, Old Mackinac Point Lighthouse has helped passing ships navigate the treacherous waters of the Straits of Mackinac since 1889. On site are authentically restored Keepers' Quarters, exhibits on lenses and fog signals, lighthouse tower tours, the film *Shipwrecks of the Straits*, and the Straits of Mackinac Shipwreck Museum.
URL: *www.mackinacparks.com*
CONTACT: mackinacparks@michigan.gov • (231) 436-4100

MANCELONA

Mancelona Historical Society Museum

ADDRESS: 9826 South Front St., Mancelona, MI 49659
ADMISSION: Contact site.
ACCESSIBILITY: Fully accessible.
DESCRIPTION: Visitors to the Mancelona Historical Society Museum can explore historical pictures and information about early days in Antrim and Mancelona, including an Emil Johnson glass-plate negative collection that consists of 60 years of photos of people from the Mancelona area.

URL: *www.ole.net/~maggie/antrim/mancy.htm*
CONTACT: sneeziecat2001@yahoo.com • (231) 676-1462

MANISTEE

Manistee County Historical Museum

ADDRESS: 425 River St., Manistee, MI 49660
ADMISSION: Charge.
ACCESSIBILITY: Partially accessible.
DESCRIPTION: The museum is owned and operated by the Manistee County Historical Society and serves to preserve, interpret, and educate the public about the history of the area. The museum is housed inside the historic 1907 Lyman Building and its permanent exhibits include seven different period rooms, maritime displays, antique dinnerware, Native-American artifacts, costumes, and dolls.

URL: *www.manisteemuseum.org*
CONTACT: manisteemuseum@gmail.com • (231) 723-5531

MAPLE CITY

Port Oneida Heritage Center

ADDRESS: 3164 W. Harbor Hwy., Maple City, MI 49664
ADMISSION: Free. Donations accepted.
ACCESSIBILITY: Partially accessible.
DESCRIPTION: The heritage center is housed at the Charles and Hattie Olsen farm—one of 21 farmsteads in the Sleeping Bear Dunes National Lakeshore's Port Oneida Rural Historic District. Visitors will find exhibits, videos, and maps that tell the story of the pioneer settlers. The family-friendly museum also offers gardens, educational programs, and biking and wagon tours.

URL: *www.phsb.org*
CONTACT: phsbpark@gmail.com • (231) 334-6103

MILLERSBURG

Millersburg Area Historical Society Museum

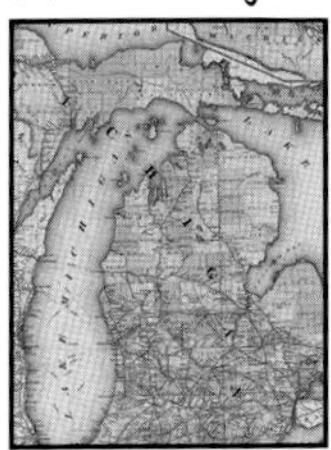

ADDRESS: 12382 Luce St., Millersburg, MI 49759
ADMISSION: Contact site.
ACCESSIBILITY: Fully accessible.
DESCRIPTION: The museum showcases artifacts from the Millersburg area in the D&M Railroad Depot, the only depot remaining in Presque Isle County. Visitors can explore photos of past residents; a model of a 1910 kitchen; artifacts; a plat book of Michigan, circa 1909; railroad memorabilia; and a map of all railroads in Michigan.

URL: *No website.*
CONTACT: (989) 733-8210

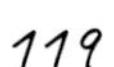

OMENA

Putnam Cloud Tower House Museum

ADDRESS: 5045 N. West Bay Shore Dr., Omena, MI 49674
ADMISSION: Free. Donations accepted.
ACCESSIBILITY: Partially accessible.
DESCRIPTION: The museum is a restored 1876 farmhouse in the Omena Historic District, listed on the National Register in 2017. Museum exhibits include baskets made by local Anishinaabek artists; photos of resort-era hotels and steamships; and rotating displays featuring aspects of local history, including an honor roll of veterans and books by Omena-area authors.
URL: *www.omenahistoricalsociety.org*
CONTACT: omenahistoricalsociety@gmail.com • (231) 386-9139

ONAWAY

Onaway Area Historical Museum

ADDRESS: 20774 State St., Onaway, MI 49765
ADMISSION: Free. Donations accepted.
ACCESSIBILITY: Fully accessible.
DESCRIPTION: The Onaway Area Historical Museum takes visitors through the history of Onaway from its lumber industry boom to its present-day status as a northern Michigan tourist destination. The museum houses many turn-of-the-twentieth-century displays including a school room, doctor's office, typical parlor, and factory-made wooden steering wheels.
URL: *www.onawayhistoricalmuseum.com*
CONTACT: onawaymuseum@gmail.com • (989) 370-8998

OSCODA

Wurtsmith Air Museum

ADDRESS: 4071 E Van Ettan St., Oscoda, MI 48750
ADMISSION: Charge.
ACCESSIBILITY: Fully accessible.
DESCRIPTION: Visit three old fighter hangars at the Oscoda Wurtsmith Airport, filled with military and aviation history. See real airplanes on display—including two that visitors may sit in. View the runway and the refueling area used by private planes, hear pilots speak over the loudspeaker, watch seven videos and a slide show, and listen to nostalgic music.
URL: *www.wurtsmithairmuseum.net*
CONTACT: email@wurtsmithairmuseum.net • (989) 739-7555

PETOSKEY

Little Traverse History Museum

ADDRESS: 100 Depot Ct., Petoskey, MI 49770
ADMISSION: Charge.
ACCESSIBILITY: Fully accessible.
DESCRIPTION: The museum focuses on the history of the Little Traverse Bay area, with displays of Petoskey stones, passenger pigeons, and train travel. Ernest Hemingway and his time spent in Northern Michigan is a particular favorite. The museum has an impressive collection of Odawa baskets and quill boxes from the nineteenth and twentieth centuries.
URL: *www.petoskeymuseum.org*
CONTACT: info@petoskeymuseum.org • (231) 347-2620

PRESQUE ISLE

Presque Isle Township Museum Society

ADDRESS: 4500 E Grand Lake Rd., Presque Isle, MI 49777
ADMISSION: Free. Donations accepted.
ACCESSIBILITY: Contact site.
DESCRIPTION: The Old Presque Isle Lighthouse, built in 1840, is adjacent to Presque Isle Harbor. In 1870, the New Presque Isle Lighthouse was built and includes a gift shop and the tallest Great Lakes light tower that the public can climb. Next door is the 1905 Keeper's House, which was fully restored by the Presque Isle Township Museum Society.
URL: *www.presqueislelighthouses.org*
CONTACT: pilighthouses@gmail.com • (989) 787-0184

ROGERS CITY

Great Lakes Lore Maritime Museum

ADDRESS: 367 N Third St., Rogers City, MI 49779
ADMISSION: Contact site.
ACCESSIBILITY: Fully accessible.
DESCRIPTION: The Great Lakes Lore Maritime Museum preserves the history of Great Lakes shipping and the people who worked the lakes. There is a large display of ship models, photographs, and artifacts. The Memorial Hall honors the crews of the *Carl D. Bradley*, S.S. *Cedarville*, *Daniel J. Morrell*, and *Edmund Fitzgerald*.
URL: *www.gllmm.com*
CONTACT: TheLoreMuseum@gmail.com • (989) 734-0706

Henry and Margaret Hoffman Annex

ADDRESS: 185 W. Michigan Ave., Rogers City, MI 49779
ADMISSION: Free. Donations accepted.
ACCESSIBILITY: Fully accessible.
DESCRIPTION: Permanent exhibits in the Hoffman Annex include histories of the Calcite Plant, the world's largest limestone quarry, and the Bradley Transportation fleet of self-unloading ships that was operated by the mining company, and one of the most extensive collections of photography equipment in the state. The Annex also contains at least one major revolving exhibit.
URL: *www.pichmuseum.org*
CONTACT: presqueislecountymuseum@gmail.com • (989) 734-0123

Presque Isle County Historical Museum

ADDRESS: 176 W. Michigan Ave., Rogers City, MI 49779
ADMISSION: Free. Donations accepted.
ACCESSIBILITY: Contact site.
DESCRIPTION: The 1914 Bradley House is part house museum and part exhibit venue. The living room, dining room, kitchen, two bathrooms, and bedroom are reminiscent of the way they might have looked in the 1930s. Other rooms in the Craftsman-style home include Native-American and pioneering exhibits and a country store, millinery shop, and one-room schoolhouse.
URL: *www.pichmuseum.org*
CONTACT: presqueislecountymuseum@gmail.com • (989) 734-0123

ROSCOMMON

Gallimore Boarding House and Museum

ADDRESS: 404 Lake St., Roscommon, MI 48653
ADMISSION: Free. Donations accepted.
ACCESSIBILITY: Partially accessible.
DESCRIPTION: The museum includes three historical buildings. The Richardson Schoolhouse is a one-room schoolhouse that serves as the actual museum housing collections from the Roscommon area. The Gallimore Boarding House was built between 1881 and 1887. The Silsby-Jacobson building—a portion of a two-story farmhouse built in 1882—contains document and picture collections.
URL: *www.visithoughtonlake.com/history.shtml*
CONTACT: (989) 344-7386

Higgins Lake Nursery and CCC Museum

ADDRESS: 11747 North Higgins Lake Dr., Roscommon, MI 48653
ADMISSION: Recreation Passport required.
ACCESSIBILITY: Fully accessible.
DESCRIPTION: More than 100,000 young men worked in Michigan's forests and parks during the Great Depression, residing in barracks like those on display at the Civilian Conservation Corps (CCC) Museum. On display are original CCC uniforms, tools, insignia, and furniture. The site is part of the Michigan History Center's Museum System.
URL: *www.michigan.gov/higginslakeccc*
CONTACT: mhcinfo@michigan.gov • (989) 348-6178

TRAVERSE CITY

Dougherty Mission House

ADDRESS: 18459 Mission Rd., Traverse City, MI 49686
ADMISSION: Charge.
ACCESSIBILITY: Fully accessible.
DESCRIPTION: The first frame house in northwest Lower Michigan was built in 1842 by Chief Agosa's tribe with Rev. Peter Dougherty. The Presbyterian Mission met terms of the 1836 Treaty of Washington. Listed on state and national registers of historic places the restored house and outbuildings appropriately reflect their history as a mission, farm, and resort from 1842 to 1917.
URL: *www.doughertyoldmissionhouse.com*
CONTACT: doughertyoldmission@yahoo.com • (269) 330-0026

Hessler Log Cabin

ADDRESS: 20500 Center Rd., Traverse City, MI 49686
ADMISSION: Free. Donations accepted.
ACCESSIBILITY: Contact site.
DESCRIPTION: Built sometime between 1854 and 1856, the log cabin was saved from demolition and moved to its present location in 1992. It is open on the fourth Sunday of June. Hear an audio tour by calling (231) 354-7550, stop #11. The cabin has a summer viewing area that allows visitors to view the interior of the building.
URL: *www.omphistoricalsociety.org*
CONTACT: info@omphistoricalsociety.org • (847) 927-5953

Maritime Heritage Alliance

ADDRESS: 13268 S. West Bayshore Dr., Traverse City, MI 49684
ADMISSION: Contact site.
ACCESSIBILITY: Partially accessible.
DESCRIPTION: At the expanding Discovery Center Campus that is shared with the Great Lakes Children's Museum we have a boat building/repair shop, a model making shop, and a self-guided display of historic wooden boats. Sailing tours are available on the reproduction schooner *Madeline* and the cutter *Champion*.

URL: *www.maritimeheritagealliance.org*
CONTACT: info@maritimeheritagealliance.org • (231) 946-2647

Old Mission Log Church

ADDRESS: Corner of Mission Rd. and Mission School Rd., Traverse City, MI 49686
ADMISSION: Free. Donations accepted.
ACCESSIBILITY: Fully accessible.
DESCRIPTION: Displays at the site share the history of the Old Mission Peninsula, including the people the Reverend Peter Dougherty met and worked with when he built the original church in 1839. The current structure is a replica of the original church. The site is open every day during the summer and year-round on the weekends.

URL: *www.omphistoricalsociety.org*
CONTACT: info@omphistoricalsociety.org • (847) 927-5953

WEST BRANCH

Ogemaw County Historical Museum

ADDRESS: 135 South Second St., West Branch, MI 48661
ADMISSION: Free. Donations accepted.
ACCESSIBILITY: Partially accessible.
DESCRIPTION: The museum includes exhibits on Native Americans, parliament wedding apparel, historic hats, local trophies, and military uniforms from past wars. A recent collection of 10,000 photos from a local photography studio is also featured. The Ogemaw County Historical Society, which operates the museum, offers driving tours of historic sites in the county.

URL: *www.ogemawcountyhistoricalsociety.com*
CONTACT: oghs1978@gmail.com • (989) 701-2525

WILLIAMSBURG

Music House Museum

ADDRESS: 7377 U.S. 31 North, Williamsburg, MI 49690
ADMISSION: Charge.
ACCESSIBILITY: Fully accessible.
DESCRIPTION: Visitors experience the sounds and history of automated instruments from the simplest music boxes through phonographs and radios. A silent movie is accompanied by the museum's mighty Wurlitzer. Tours provide visitors with a musical journey through the sounds, artistry, history, and science of the early forerunners to our modern-day music sources.

URL: *www.musichouse.org*
CONTACT: info@musichouse.org • (231) 938-9300

UPPER PENINSULA REGION

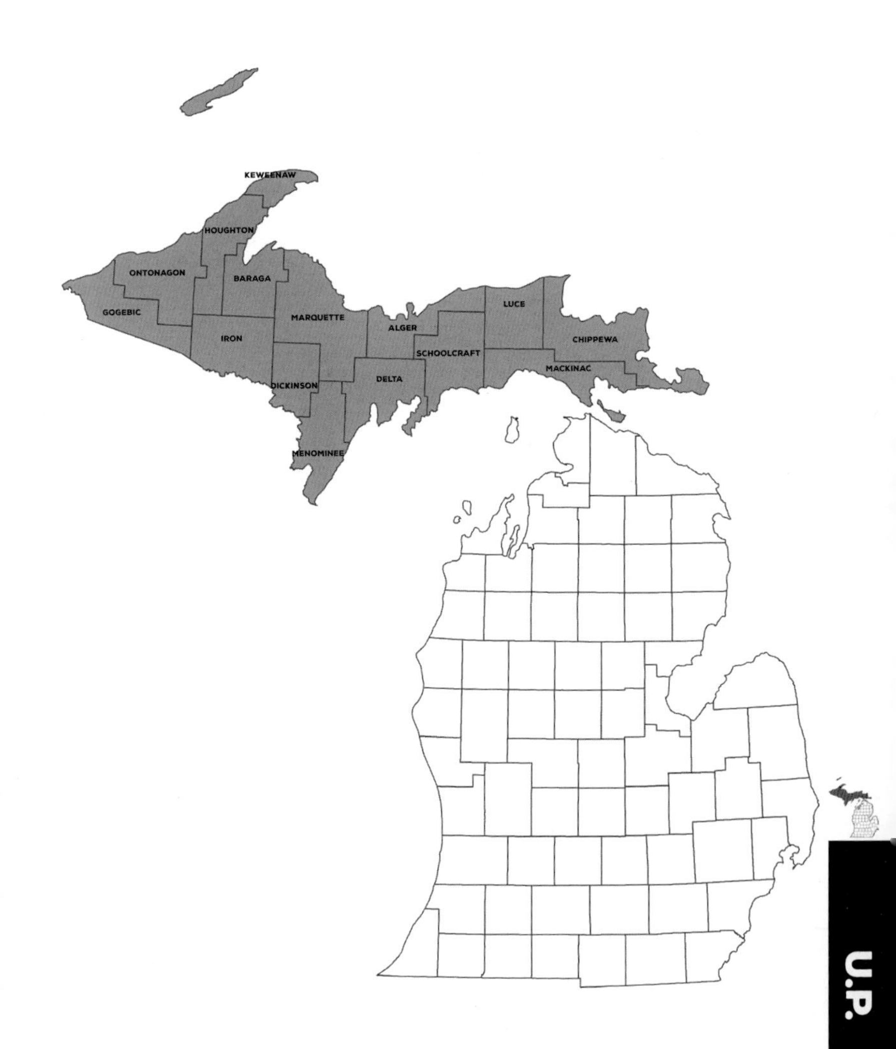

ALPHA

Alpha Historical Museum

ADDRESS: 303 Center St., Alpha, MI 49902
ADMISSION: Free. Donations accepted.
ACCESSIBILITY: Fully accessible.
DESCRIPTION: Located within a 1914 First National Bank building, the museum includes items relating to the village of Alpha and surrounding area, such as a film of local major events, a gallery of Porter School senior class photos, images and trophies highlighting student excellence, memorabilia from local veterans, and displays of mining and farming history.
URL: *Facebook: Alpha Mastadon Historical Society*
CONTACT: alphamastodon@gmail.com • (906) 875-4313

BARAGA

Baraga County Historical Museum

ADDRESS: 803 US Hwy. 41, Baraga, MI 49908
ADMISSION: Charge.
ACCESSIBILITY: Fully accessible.
DESCRIPTION: Located adjacent to beautiful Keweenaw Bay, the Baraga County Historical Museum offers a variety of exhibits highlighting significant events in local history, as well as illustrating what life was like years ago. RV parking is available, and a picnic area between the museum and the lakeshore provides a place for visitors to relax before or after touring the museum itself.
URL: *www.baragacountyhistoricalmuseum.com*
CONTACT: baragacountyhistory@gmail.com • (906) 353-8444

BESSEMER

Bessemer Area Historical Society and Heritage Center

ADDRESS: 403 S. Sophie St., Bessemer, MI 49911
ADMISSION: Free. Donations accepted.
ACCESSIBILITY: Fully accessible.
DESCRIPTION: Visitors can also see exhibits on mining, logging, sawmills, railroads, education, farming, veterans, clothing, and household items. In addition, various historical slideshows and DVDs are available for viewing, while local historical publications can be purchased in the Heritage Center store.
URL: *www.bessemerhistory.org*
CONTACT: bessemerhistory@gmail.com • (906) 663-4372

BRIMLEY

Point Iroquois Lighthouse

ADDRESS: 13042-13260 W. Lakeshore Dr., Brimley, MI 49715
ADMISSION: Contact site.
ACCESSIBILITY: Partially accessible.
DESCRIPTION: The lighthouse is owned and operated by the USDA Forest Service with the help of the Bay Mills-Brimley Historical Research Society. The museum reveals the stories of the lighthouse keepers and their families through family album photographs, antiques, and artifacts. Climb the 72 steps to the top of the tower for a picturesque view of Lake Superior.
URL: *www.fs.usda.gov/attmain/hiawatha/specialplaces*
CONTACT: HiawathaNF@fs.fed.us • (906) 437-5272

Wheels of History Train Museum

ADDRESS: 6799 Depot St., Brimley, MI 49715
ADMISSION: Free. Donations accepted.
ACCESSIBILITY: Partially accessible.
DESCRIPTION: The Wheels of History Train Museum is located in an 1897 Replica Depot and offers changing exhibits. The main collections include exhibits of maps, photos, and artifacts of one-room schools, the lumber industry, railroad history, early life in the area, and veterans' memorabilia and uniforms.

URL: *Facebook: Wheels of History Train Museum*
CONTACT: paulinerice1@yahoo.com • (906) 248-3665

CALUMET

Copper Country Firefighters History Museum

ADDRESS: 327 Sixth St., Calumet, MI 49913
ADMISSION: Charge.
ACCESSIBILITY: Partially accessible.
DESCRIPTION: Firefighting equipment spanning 175 years is on display, including five running trucks from 1919 to 1950 and fire department shoulder patches from around Michigan and other states. There is an exhibit on the Italian Hall Tragedy in which 73 people, mostly children, died on Christmas Eve 1913, when someone yelled "FIRE!" It was a false alarm.

URL: *Facebook: Copper Country Firefighters History Museum*
CONTACT: coppercountryfirefighters@hotmail.com • (906) 337-4579

Keweenaw National Historical Park

ADDRESS: 98 5th St., Calumet, MI 49913
ADMISSION: Free. Donations accepted.
ACCESSIBILITY: Fully accessible.
DESCRIPTION: Keweenaw National Historic Park tells of nation's first mineral rush and the people it brought from around the world. The Calumet Visitor Center sheds light on the social and cultural history of Keweenaw's copper boom, while 21 Keweenaw Heritage Sites—from underground mines to ghost towns to museums—provide further experiences relating to the region's mining past.

URL: *www.nps.gov/kewe*
CONTACT: kewe_information@nps.gov • (906) 337-3168

Norwegian Lutheran Church

ADDRESS: 608 Elm St., Calumet, MI 49913
ADMISSION: Contact site.
ACCESSIBILITY: Contact site.
DESCRIPTION: The Norwegian Lutheran Church Historical Society was founded in 2000 to restore and maintain the historic 1898 Norwegian Lutheran Church. The building contains the original altar, pews, organ, chandelier, and tin ceiling. Storyboards share the church's history, a list of its ministers, and photos of church individuals.

URL: *www.nlc-calumet.org*
CONTACT: info@nlc-calumet.org • (906) 337-3731

CASPIAN

Iron County Historical Society & Museum

ADDRESS: 100 Brady Ave., Caspian, MI 49915
ADMISSION: Free. Donations accepted.
ACCESSIBILITY: Partially accessible.
DESCRIPTION: Founded in 1962, the museum grounds include a log cabin, lumber camp, mine site, the Carrie Jacobs-Bond Home, a pioneer schoolhouse, Toti's Tavern, Stager Depot, and more. There are two galleries: the LeBlanc Wildlife Art Gallery and the Giovanelli Studio & Gallery. The museum's 100-plus displays depict Iron County history including mining, logging, and homesteading.
URL: *www.ironcountymuseum.org*
CONTACT: info@ironcountymuseum.org • (906) 265-2617

CHASSELL

Chassell Heritage Center

ADDRESS: 42373 N Hancock St., Chassell, MI 49916
ADMISSION: Free. Donations accepted.
ACCESSIBILITY: Contact site.
DESCRIPTION: The Chassell Historical Organization maintains its township museum in a former elementary school. Exhibits include stories of Finnish and French-Canadian immigrants engaged in commercial fishing, logging and lumber milling, and agriculture. Furthermore, the heritage center highlights local school history and houses the Friends of Fashion vintage clothing collection.
URL: *www.chassellhistory.org*
CONTACT: info@chassellhistory.org • (906) 523-1155

COPPER HARBOR

Fort Wilkins Historic Complex & Copper Harbor Lighthouse

ADDRESS: 15223 U.S. 41, Copper Harbor, MI 49918
ADMISSION: Recreation Passport required.
ACCESSIBILITY: Partially accessible.
DESCRIPTION: Opened in 1844, Fort Wilkins was a U.S. Army post on the northern Keweenaw Peninsula. The site contains barracks, officer's quarters, a sutler's store, and more. Every summer, a living history program allows visitors to experience what life was like at the fort. The park also includes the Copper Harbor lighthouses. The site is part of the Michigan History Center's Museum System.
URL: *www.michigan.gov/ftwilkins*
CONTACT: mhcinfo@michigan.gov • (906) 289-4215

CRYSTAL FALLS

Harbour House Museum

ADDRESS: 17 North Fourth St., Crystal Falls, MI 49920
ADMISSION: Charge.
ACCESSIBILITY: Fully accessible.
DESCRIPTION: The former Harbour family home was built at the turn of the twentieth century and features a unique architectural steamboat-style construction. The first floor replicates a way of life during the early 1900s while the upstairs rooms have information on mining, military, and railroad history, and other local history subjects.
URL: *www.crystalfallsmuseum-harbourhouse.org*
CONTACT: cfharbourhouse@gmail.com • (906) 284-3405

DE TOUR VILLAGE

De Tour Passage Historical Museum

ADDRESS: 104 Elizabeth St., De Tour Village, MI 49725
ADMISSION: Contact site.
ACCESSIBILITY: Fully accessible.
DESCRIPTION: Visit the museum to see one of the few rare third-order Fresnel lenses. Also featured are many photos and displays depicting local lighthouses, ferries, early ship refueling docks, the history of local fishing and sawmills, early settlers, and Native Americans.

URL: *Facebook: De Tour Passage Historical Museum*
CONTACT: myreoffice@yahoo.com • (906) 297-2081

DRUMMOND ISLAND

De Tour Reef Light

ADDRESS: Mouth of the St. Mary's River, Between De Tour Village and Drummond Island, Drummond Island, MI 49726
ADMISSION: Charge.
ACCESSIBILITY: Contact site.
DESCRIPTION: Come experience the distinctive architectural characteristics of an early-twentieth-century Great Lakes crib-foundation lighthouse. Located where the St. Marys River joins Lake Huron at the south end of DeTour Passage, the lighthouse has been an important aid to navigation throughout its existence.

URL: *www.drlps.com*
CONTACT: drlps@drlps.com • (906) 493-6609

EAGLE HARBOR

Commercial Fishing Museum

ADDRESS: Eagle Harbor Lighthouse Complex, 670 Lighthouse Rd., Eagle Harbor, MI 49950
ADMISSION: Charge.
ACCESSIBILITY: Contact site.
DESCRIPTION: Visitors can see displays of commercial fishing activities across the Keweenaw and of the various generations that fished. The impressive collection of photographs in the museum puts a human face on the rough and risky business of commercial fishing in Lake Superior and shows the related history of copper mining in the area.

URL: *www.keweenawhistory.org*
CONTACT: Contact via website. • (906) 289-4990

Eagle Harbor Lifesaving Station

ADDRESS: End of Marina Rd., Eagle Harbor, MI 49950
ADMISSION: Free. Donations accepted.
ACCESSIBILITY: Contact site.
DESCRIPTION: Once a separate governmental agency, the Lifesaving Service became part of the U.S. Coast Guard in 1915. To honor these brave men and their families, the Lifesaving Station Museum was opened in the old Life Saving Station boathouse near the marina in Eagle Harbor. The museum displays early wooden rescue boats and a completely restored 26-foot Pulling Surfboat.

URL: *www.keweenawhistory.org*
CONTACT: Contact via website. • (906) 289-4990

Eagle Harbor Lighthouse

ADDRESS: 670 Lighthouse Rd., Eagle Harbor, MI 49950
ADMISSION: Charge.
ACCESSIBILITY: Contact site.
DESCRIPTION: Tour one of the Keweenaw's most photographed lighthouses, which has been operating since 1871 and has restored living quarters and a Fresnel lens on display. The top of the tower is not open because the U.S. Coast Guard continues to operate the light at the top of the tower as an active navigational aid.
URL: *www.keweenawhistory.org/Eagle-Harbor-Lighthouse*
CONTACT: Contact via website. • (906) 289-4990

Keweenaw History Museum

ADDRESS: Eagle Harbor Lighthouse Complex, 670 Lighthouse Rd., Eagle Harbor, MI 49950
ADMISSION: Charge.
ACCESSIBILITY: Fully accessible.
DESCRIPTION: The museum is located in the old Coast Guard garage building. The history of mining is displayed through photographs and artifacts that trace the 6,000 year old history of mining in the Keweenaw. The wreck of the S.S. *Bangor* in 1926 near Copper Harbor and its load of Chrysler automobiles is examined in detail.
URL: *www.keweenawhistory.org*
CONTACT: Contact via website. • (906) 289-4990

Maritime Museum

ADDRESS: Eagle Harbor Lighthouse Complex, 670 Lighthouse Rd., Eagle Harbor, MI 49950
ADMISSION: Charge.
ACCESSIBILITY: Fully accessible.
DESCRIPTION: The museum is inside of the old Fog Signal Building and contains displays that look at the role of shipping on Lake Superior. The museum has several scale models of ships, stories of many of the ships that sailed Lake Superior and of several shipwrecks, navigation displays, maritime equipment, and a working marine radio.
URL: *www.keweenawhistory.org*
CONTACT: Contact via website. • (906) 289-4990

Rathbone School/Knights of Pythias Museum

ADDRESS: 277 Center St., Eagle Harbor, MI 49950
ADMISSION: Free. Donations accepted.
ACCESSIBILITY: Contact site.
DESCRIPTION: The Rathbone School served the Eagle Harbor community from 1853 to 1872. Justus Rathbone was a teacher and also the founder of the Knights of Pythias, a secret fraternal society. Presently, one side of the building is set up as a one-room school and the other side contains memorabilia commemorating the Knights of Pythias.
URL: *www.keweenawhistory.org*
CONTACT: Contact via website. • (906) 289-4990

EAGLE RIVER

Eagle River Museum

ADDRESS: 5059 4th St., Eagle River, MI 49924
ADMISSION: Free. Donations accepted.
ACCESSIBILITY: Partially accessible.
DESCRIPTION: The Eagle River Museum is in the old Eagle River School building which now serves as the Houghton Township Community Building near the waterfall and dam. The exhibits tell the stories of the Clifton and Eagle River communities and the pioneers who settled these communities. Volunteer docents are available on site.
URL: *www.keweenawhistory.org*
CONTACT: Contact via website. • (906) 289-4990

ENGADINE

Engadine Historical Museum

ADDRESS: 14075 Melville St., Engadine, MI 49827
ADMISSION: Free. Donations accepted.
ACCESSIBILITY: Partially accessible.
DESCRIPTION: The museum, located in the former Hastings House, reflects life in the community dating back to 1894. With a focus on lumbering and agriculture, displays include an 1895 restored and furnished log house, one-room schoolhouse replica, military artifacts, Country Bank vault, and objects from the cooperage mill, which was the community's largest employer at the time.
URL: *www.sites.google.com/view/engadinehistoricalmuseum*
CONTACT: engadinehistorical@gmail.com • (906) 477-6908

ESCANABA

Delta County Historical Museum

ADDRESS: 16 Beaumier Way, Escanaba, MI 49829
ADMISSION: Contact site.
ACCESSIBILITY: Partially accessible.
DESCRIPTION: Exhibits portray many aspects of the area's history, including logging, shipping, the railroad industry, military, Native-American culture, surveying, sports, fishing, local businesses, and much more. A new building now contains the museum and the archives. The society also maintains Sand Point Lighthouse. The lighthouse home, tower, and boathouse are open to visitors.
URL: *www.deltahistorical.org*
CONTACT: arch@deltahistorical.org • (906) 789-6790

GARDEN

Fayette Historic Townsite

ADDRESS: 4785 II Rd., Garden, MI 49835
ADMISSION: Recreation Passport required.
ACCESSIBILITY: Contact site.
DESCRIPTION: This well-preserved museum village of 19 historic structures, recalls a time when it was a noisy, bustling, iron-smelting town with an immigrant population that shared daily hardships and comforts. Visitors can also enjoy the serenity of a Lake Michigan harbor, white dolomite bluffs, and verdant forests. The site is part of the Michigan History Center's Museum System.
URL: *www.michigan.gov/fayettetownsite*
CONTACT: mhcinfo@michigan.gov • (906) 644-2603

GAY

Historic School at Gay

ADDRESS: Lake St. and Gay Rd., Gay, MI 49950
ADMISSION: Free. Donations accepted.
ACCESSIBILITY: Partially accessible.
DESCRIPTION: Restored and operated by the Keweenaw County Historical Society, the Historic School at Gay conveys the impact of the commercial lumber, fishing, and mining mills on the town of Gay and the environment. The first school was built in 1902 to meet the needs of the mill workers' families, but after overcrowding, a larger two-story building was constructed in 1927.
URL: *www.keweenawhistory.org*
CONTACT: Contact via website. • (906) 289-4990

GRAND MARAIS

Lightkeeper's House Museum

ADDRESS: Coast Guard Point Rd., Grand Marais, MI 49839
ADMISSION: Contact site.
ACCESSIBILITY: Contact site.
DESCRIPTION: The Grand Marais Lightkeeper's House dates to 1906 and has been restored to its original appearance as the lightkeeper's home of the early 1900s. Period furniture and artifacts are on display. Museum T-shirts, sweatshirts, mugs, historical society publications, and historical prints and postcards are available.
URL: *www.grandmaraismichigan.com/visit-us/attractions/museums/*
CONTACT: gmhistoricalsociety@gmail.com • (906) 494-2570

Old Post Office Museum

ADDRESS: N14272 Lake Ave., Grand Marais, MI 49839
ADMISSION: Contact site.
ACCESSIBILITY: Fully accessible.
DESCRIPTION: The Old Post Office Museum, operated by the Grand Marais Historical Society, showcases the history of Grand Marais and the surrounding area inside the former town post office. Displays and artifacts detail the various eras of the town's past, from early Native-American settlements to the present day.
URL: *www.grandmaraismichigan.com/visit-us/attractions/museums/*
CONTACT: gmhistoricalsociety@gmail.com • (906) 494-2570

Pickle Barrel House Museum

ADDRESS: Intersection of Lake Ave. and Randolph St., Grand Marais, MI 49839
ADMISSION: Contact site.
ACCESSIBILITY: Partially accessible.
DESCRIPTION: Run by the Grand Marais Historical Society, the Pickle Barrel House Museum is a unique barrel-shaped structure that has been restored to look as it did in the 1930s. The two-story front barrel has a living area with a bedroom upstairs, and is connected via a pantry to the single-story kitchen barrel at the rear.
URL: *www.grandmaraismichigan.com/visit-us/attractions/museums/*
CONTACT: gmhistoricalsociety@gmail.com • (906) 494-2570

GWINN

Forsyth Township Historical Society Museum

ADDRESS: 184 West Flint St., Gwinn, MI 49841
ADMISSION: Contact site.
ACCESSIBILITY: Contact site.
DESCRIPTION: The museum showcases the history of the township's small mining and railroad villages from the 1860s as well as the history of K.I. Sawyer Air Force Base. There's a special emphasis on the unique "model town" of Gwinn, built in 1908 by Cleveland-Cliffs Iron Company President William Gwinn Mather. The museum is located above Forsyth Township Hall.
URL: *Facebook: Forsyth Township Historical Society*
CONTACT: rpwills@yahoo.com • (906) 346-5413

HANCOCK

Quincy Mine

ADDRESS: 49750 US Hwy. 41, Hancock, MI 49930
ADMISSION: Charge.
ACCESSIBILITY: Partially accessible.
DESCRIPTION: The mine serves as a gateway into the Copper Country's rich heritage. Utilizing its unique historical resources—its historic mining location, buildings, equipment and underground mine—as well as high-quality interpretive tours, exhibits and programming, the Quincy Mine site provides an engaging and educational visitor experience.
URL: *www.quincymine.com*
CONTACT: info@quincymine.com • (906) 482-5569

HERMANSVILLE

IXL Historical Museum

ADDRESS: W5551 River St. N., Hermansville, MI 49847
ADMISSION: Contact site.
ACCESSIBILITY: Partially accessible.
DESCRIPTION: The museum consists of the original 1880s office building of the Wisconsin Land and Lumber Company and IXL Flooring Company of Hermansville. The main building contains four floors of lumber artifacts as well as estate furnishings. Other buildings on site include the Hermansville Produce Warehouse, the IXL Carriage House, a company house, a train depot, and a caboose.
URL: *Facebook: IXL Historical Museum*
CONTACT: ixlmuseum1882@gmail.com • (906) 236-5163

HOUGHTON

A.E. Seaman Mineral Museum

ADDRESS: 1404 E. Sharon Ave., Houghton, MI 49931
ADMISSION: Charge.
ACCESSIBILITY: Fully accessible.
DESCRIPTION: Since its inception in 1902, the A.E. Seaman Mineral Museum has housed one of the premiere crystal collections in North America and has showcased the world's finest display of minerals from Michigan's famous Lake Superior Copper District. Because of this, in 1990 the Michigan State legislature designated the museum as the "official Mineralogical Museum of Michigan."
URL: *www.museum.mtu.edu*
CONTACT: museum@mtu.edu • (906) 487-2572

Carnegie Museum of the Keweenaw

ADDRESS: 105 Huron St., Houghton, MI 49931
ADMISSION: Free. Donations accepted.
ACCESSIBILITY: Partially accessible.
DESCRIPTION: The Carnegie Museum of the Keweenaw is housed in the former 1910 Houghton Public Library. Since the museum was established in 2007, the building has undergone several renovation projects to return it to its 1910 grandeur, while re-purposing it as a twenty-first-century museum. In addition, a public Community Room complete with a stage, screen, and projector is available.
URL: *www.carnegiekeweenaw.org*
CONTACT: history@cityofhoughton.com • (906) 482-7140

IRON MOUNTAIN

Cornish Pumping Engine & Mining Museum

ADDRESS: 300 Kent St., Iron Mountain, MI 49801
ADMISSION: Charge.
ACCESSIBILITY: Fully accessible.
DESCRIPTION: The Cornish Pumping Engine & Mining Museum features artifacts from Menominee Iron Range history, an exhibit on the Iron Mountain Ford Motor Company plant, and displays on area logging and lumbering. It also includes one of North America's largest steam engines—weighing 725 tons, standing 54 feet tall, and pumping 3,190 gallons of water per minute.
URL: *www.menomineemuseum.com*
CONTACT: mrhmuseum@gmail.com • (906) 774-1086

Menominee Range Historical Museum

ADDRESS: 411 Kent St., Iron Mountain, MI 49801
ADMISSION: Charge.
ACCESSIBILITY: Fully accessible.
DESCRIPTION: The museum features exhibits depicting local history from Native-American inhabitants through the early years of the twentieth century. Re-created period interiors, including a general store, Ojibwa wigwam, blacksmith's shop, jewelry and cobbler shops, various medical offices, and horse-drawn vehicles, help to tell the story of the Menominee Range.
URL: *www.menomineemuseum.com*
CONTACT: mrhmuseum@gmail.com • (906) 774-1086

World War II Glider and Military Museum

ADDRESS: 302 Kent St., Iron Mountain, MI 49801
ADMISSION: Charge.
ACCESSIBILITY: Fully accessible.
DESCRIPTION: This Menominee Range Historical Foundation operates the museum which features a CG-4A glider—one of seven restored gliders worldwide—that was produced by Iron Mountain's Ford Motor Company plant. Other collections include military uniforms from the Civil War to Desert Storm, historic photos and footage, and numerous historical automobiles.
URL: *www.menomineemuseum.com*
CONTACT: (906) 774-1086

IRON RIVER

Beechwood Hall

ADDRESS: 178 Beechwood Store Rd., Iron River, MI 49935
ADMISSION: Free. Donations accepted.
ACCESSIBILITY: Fully accessible.
DESCRIPTION: The former Beechwood School maintains the features of a rural one-room schoolhouse. It houses temporary historical exhibits and a growing collection of art and photographs depicting life in Beechwood, which is on the list of Michigan ghost towns.

URL: *Facebook: Beechwood Historical Society*
CONTACT: beechwoodhistoricalsociety@gmail.com • No phone listed.

IRONWOOD

Erwin Township Historical Society Museum

ADDRESS: 8970 Van Buskirk Rd., Ironwood, MI 49938
ADMISSION: Free. Donations accepted.
ACCESSIBILITY: Fully accessible.
DESCRIPTION: The East End School, a one-room schoolhouse, was purchased, moved to Erwin Heritage Park, and completely restored—becoming a museum, research library, and meeting space. The park features a paved walking trail and there are plans to create a historical walk-along on the trail system and a children's playground.

URL: *Facebook: Erwin Township Historical Society*
CONTACT: erwintownshiphistoricalsociety@gmail.com

Historic Ironwood Depot

ADDRESS: 150 N. Lowell St., Ironwood, MI 49938
ADMISSION: Free. Donations accepted.
ACCESSIBILITY: Fully accessible.
DESCRIPTION: Headquartered in the Historic Ironwood Depot—which is on the National Register of Historic Places—the Ironwood Area Historical Society maintains a museum and gift shop. Its exhibits are focused on life and mining on the Gogebic Range as well as the area's lumbering and railroading past.

URL: *Facebook: Ironwood Area Historical Society*
CONTACT: ironwoodhistoricalsociety@gmail.com • (906) 932-0287

Ironwood Memorial Building

ADDRESS: 213 S. Marquette St., Ironwood, MI 49938
ADMISSION: Free. Donations accepted.
ACCESSIBILITY: Fully accessible.
DESCRIPTION: The Ironwood Memorial Building houses a self-guided tour of Ironwood history. See early mining and logging exhibits and artifacts. The structure was built in 1922 and is listed on the National Register of Historic Places. A brochure is available to help visitors explore two floors of displays and historical photo exhibits.

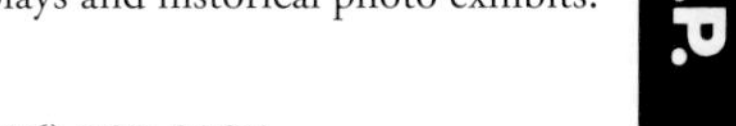

URL: *Facebook: Ironwood Area Historical Society*
CONTACT: ironwoodhistoricalsociety@gmail.com • (906) 932-0287

ISHPEMING

Cliffs Shaft Mining Museum

ADDRESS: 501 West Euclid St., Ishpeming, MI 49849
ADMISSION: Charge.
ACCESSIBILITY: Partially accessible.
DESCRIPTION: Cliffs Shaft Mining Museum is known for having a well-preserved example of underground iron mining in Michigan. Other items to explore include mining artifacts, railroad artifacts, Ispheming rock, and more than 700 mineral specimens. In addition, visitors can view historical displays of miners and mines.

URL: *www.cliffsshaftminemuseum.com*
CONTACT: cliffsshaft18@gmail.com • (906) 485-1882

Ishpeming Area Historical Society Museum

ADDRESS: 308 Cleveland Ave., Ste. 305 Ishpeming, MI 49849
ADMISSION: Contact site.
ACCESSIBILITY: Fully accessible.
DESCRIPTION: Discover some of Ishpeming's legends—like John Voelker, Kelly Johnson, and Glenn Seaborg—at the Ishpeming Area Historical Society Museum. It features early city documents, *Anatomy of a Murder* memorabilia, historical Gossard building artifacts, music history, and military uniforms. The museum also offers a treasure hunt for children.

URL: *www.ishpeminghistory.org*
CONTACT: ishphistoricalsociety@gmail.com • (906) 486-8680

LAKE LINDEN

Houghton County Historical Society Museum

ADDRESS: 53102 Hwy. M-26, Lake Linden, MI 49945
ADMISSION: Free. Donations accepted.
ACCESSIBILITY: Partially accessible.
DESCRIPTION: Exhibits include Lake Linden & Torch Lake Railroad as well as a steam locomotive and a three-foot-gauge track to support tours interpreting the former Calumet and Hecla Mill. Trains run during weekends. The site also houses a general history museum, a 1940s log cabin, a schoolhouse, and the former First Congressional Church of Lake Linden with a restored pipe organ.

URL: *www.houghtonhistory.org*
CONTACT: info@houghtonhistory.org • (906) 296-4121

MACKINAC ISLAND

Fort Mackinac

ADDRESS: 7127 Huron Rd., Mackinac Island, MI 49757
ADMISSION: Charge.
ACCESSIBILITY: Partially accessible.
DESCRIPTION: Fort Mackinac includes 14 original buildings, including one of Michigan's oldest buildings: the officers' stone quarters, which dates back to 1780. Through exhibits, visitors learn about life at the fort, including military training, battles, medical treatments, and family life.

URL: *www.mackinacparks.com*
CONTACT: mackinacparks@michigan.gov • (231) 436-4100

Richard and Jane Manoogian Mackinac Art Museum

ADDRESS: 7070 Main St., Mackinac Island, MI 49757
ADMISSION: Charge.
ACCESSIBILITY: Partially accessible.
DESCRIPTION: One of the most diverse art museums in the region, the site allows visitors to experience fine and decorative arts inspired by Mackinac through the ages. From hand-beaded Native-American garments and seventeenth- and eighteenth-century maps of the Great Lakes to one-of-a-kind pieces from the height of Mackinac Island's Victorian era.
URL: *www.mackinacparks.com*
CONTACT: mackinacparks@michigan.gov • (231) 436-4100

MACKINAW CITY

St. Helena Island Light Station

ADDRESS: 707 North Huron Ave., Mackinaw City, MI 49701
ADMISSION: Contact site.
ACCESSIBILITY: Contact site.
DESCRIPTION: The St. Helena Island Light Station is a fully restored light station with a live-in volunteer keeper program. The Great Lakes Lighthouse Keepers Association offers workshops in residence at St. Helena Island Light Station in Northern Michigan's Straits of Mackinac. Boat access only, contact site if you want to visit using your own boat.
URL: *www.gllka.org*
CONTACT: info@gllka.com • (231) 436-5580

MANISTIQUE

Schoolcraft County Historical Society Museum

ADDRESS: Pioneer Park-Deer St., Manistique, MI 49854
ADMISSION: Contact site.
ACCESSIBILITY: Partially accessible.
DESCRIPTION: The Schoolcraft County Historical Society Museum is located in a small 1910 house and includes exhibits from the 1890s. The fire engine building contains a hook-and-ladder truck from the 1800s as well as a 1950 La France Fire Truck. The Manistique Water Tower, circa 1923, is open and contains special exhibits for visitors of all ages.
URL: *www.schs.cityofmanistique.org*
CONTACT: schs1860@gmail.com

MARQUETTE

Baraga Educational Center and Museum

ADDRESS: 615 S. Fourth St., Marquette, MI 49855
ADMISSION: Free. Donations accepted.
ACCESSIBILITY: Fully accessible.
DESCRIPTION: The Baraga Educational Center and Museum is also a gift shop and pilgrimage site. Located on the first floor of the Baraga House, the museum contains artifacts from the life and labor of the Venerable Bishop Frederic Baraga—the first bishop of the Roman Catholic Diocese of Marquette and a current candidate for sainthood.
URL: *www.bishopbaraga.org*
CONTACT: bishopbaragaassoc@gmail.com • (906) 227-9117

Beaumier U.P. Heritage Center

ADDRESS: 1401 Presque Ave., Gries Hall Marquette, MI 49855
ADMISSION: Free. Donations accepted.
ACCESSIBILITY: Contact site.
DESCRIPTION: The Beaumier U.P. Heritage Center is dedicated to telling and celebrating the history and culture of the Upper Peninsula. Located in Gries Hall on the campus of Northern Michigan University, the center features regularly changing exhibits in its main gallery along with displays throughout the campus.
URL: *www.nmu.edu/beaumierheritagecenter*
CONTACT: heritage@nmu.edu • (906) 227-3212

Marquette Maritime Museum

ADDRESS: 300 North Lakeshore Blvd., Marquette, MI 49855
ADMISSION: Charge.
ACCESSIBILITY: Partially accessible.
DESCRIPTION: The Marquette Maritime Museum is one of the Upper Peninsula's best kept secrets. The museum features exhibits on Marquette and Lake Superior shipwrecks, the U.S. Coast Guard, a 3-D breeches buoy display, as well as one of the largest collections of Fresnel lenses on the Great Lakes. The gift shop features nautical gifts such as books, t-shirts, magnets, and mugs.
URL: *www.mqtmaritimemuseum.com*
CONTACT: mqtmaritimemanager@gmail.com • (906) 226-2006

Marquette Regional History Center

ADDRESS: 145 W Spring St., Marquette, MI 49855
ADMISSION: Charge.
ACCESSIBILITY: Fully accessible.
DESCRIPTION: The center contains an extensive permanent exhibit, rotating special exhibit, and research library. The permanent collection includes artifacts from the Prehistoric copper culture through contemporary times. Only a fraction of the permanent collection is on display at one time. Ongoing special exhibits allow the museum to highlight different areas of the collection.
URL: *www.marquettehistory.org*
CONTACT: mrhc@marquettehistory.org • (906) 226-3571

MENOMINEE

Menominee Heritage Museum

ADDRESS: 904 11th Ave., Menominee, MI 49858
ADMISSION: Free. Donations accepted.
ACCESSIBILITY: Fully accessible.
DESCRIPTION: At the Heritage Museum, the history of Menominee County is displayed. Visitors will find stories shown through photos and artifacts that range from Native-American canoes to opera house chairs. The museum is located in the former St. John the Baptist Catholic Church. This building is listed on the National Register of Historic Places.
URL: *www.menomineehistory.org*
CONTACT: menomineeheritagemuseum@gmail.com • (906) 863-9000

West Shore Fishing Museum

ADDRESS: N5146 State Highway M35, Menominee, MI 49858
ADMISSION: Contact site.
ACCESSIBILITY: Fully accessible.
DESCRIPTION: West Shore Fishing Museum is a homestead museum portraying the life of a commercial fishing family. Situated on 24-acres of scenic waterfront, the museum offers a restored home built in the 1890s, two exhibit buildings, outdoor displays of five commercial fishing vessels, a vintage gift shop, about three miles of walking trails with shore access, and lovely gardens and grounds.
URL: *Facebook: West Shore Fishing Museum*
CONTACT: wsfmuseum@gmail.com • (715) 923-9756

MICHIGAMME

Michigamme Museum

ADDRESS: 110 West Main St., Michigamme, MI 49861
ADMISSION: Free. Donations accepted.
ACCESSIBILITY: Contact site.
DESCRIPTION: The Michigamme Museum contains more than 150 years of local history told through artifacts, memorabilia, and antiques. Highlights include displays on Henry Ford, Dr. VanRiper, the town's famous Moose Lift, and the filming of *Anatomy of a Murder*. The museum also houses a 1900 American LaFrance steam fire engine and a collection of gravesite listings and obituaries.
URL: *www.michigammetownship.com*
CONTACT: michigammetownship@gmail.com • (906) 323-9016

MOHAWK

Central Mine

ADDRESS: 7413 Central Rd., Mohawk, MI 49950
ADMISSION: Free. Donations accepted.
ACCESSIBILITY: Partially accessible.
DESCRIPTION: Walk the "ghost town" of Central, once the home of over 1,200 people and site of a copper mine, which closed in 1898. Three buildings are open to visitors, including the Central Visitor Center, which provides interpretive exhibits about the mine, the miners' families, home, schools and churches.
URL: *www.keweenawhistory.org*
CONTACT: Contact via website. • (906) 289-4990

MUNISING

Alger County Historical Society Museum

ADDRESS: 1496 Washington St., Munising, MI 49862
ADMISSION: Contact site.
ACCESSIBILITY: Fully accessible.
DESCRIPTION: In 1993, the Alger County Historical Society opened its heritage center in the former Washington Grade School. Exhibits cover history of historic Grand Island and the Grand Island Recreation Area, Munising Woodenware Company, barn-building, homemaking, Native Americans, and sauna. There is also a fur trader's cabin and blacksmith shop on site.
URL: *Facebook: Alger County Historical Society and Heritage Center*
CONTACT: algerchs@jamadots.com • (906) 387-4308

NAUBINWAY

Top of the Lake Snowmobile Museum

ADDRESS: W11660 US 2, Naubinway, MI 49762
ADMISSION: Charge.
ACCESSIBILITY: Fully accessible.
DESCRIPTION: The museum instantly transforms visitors back in time to the era of snowmobiling when it first began, to the era of the sport machine when there were more than 200 manufacturers, and also to the racing era. Visitors will see snowmobile memorabilia and its history; dealer signs hanging from the ceiling; and helmets, suits, and gloves that "grandpa" wore.
URL: *www.snowmobilemuseum.com*
CONTACT: info@snowmobilemuseum.com • (906) 477-6298

NEGAUNEE

Michigan Iron Industry Museum

ADDRESS: 73 Forge Rd., Negaunee, MI 49866
ADMISSION: Free. Donations accepted.
ACCESSIBILITY: Fully accessible.
DESCRIPTION: Amid the forested ravines of the Marquette Iron Range, the Michigan Iron Industry Museum overlooks the Carp River and the site of the first iron forge in the Lake Superior region. The museum's exhibits highlight the state's iron-mining industry—which has flourished for more than 125 years—and interpret everyday life in mining communities.
URL: *www.michigan.gov/mhc/museums/miim*
CONTACT: mhcinfo@michigan.gov • (906) 475-7857

Negaunee Historical Museum

ADDRESS: 303 East Main St., Negaunee, MI 49866
ADMISSION: Free. Donations accepted.
ACCESSIBILITY: Contact site.
DESCRIPTION: The museum, operated by the Negaunee Historical Society, features three floors of exhibits focusing on mining, industries supporting mining activities, business, architecture, schools, athletics, entertainment, and the rich heritage of groups of people who settled in the area.
URL: *www.negauneehistory.org*
CONTACT: negauneehistory@gmail.com • (906) 475-4614

NEWBERRY

Luce County Historical Museum

ADDRESS: 411 West Harrie St., Newberry, MI 49869
ADMISSION: Free. Donations accepted.
ACCESSIBILITY: Fully accessible.
DESCRIPTION: The Luce County Historical Museum is in the former sheriff's residence and jail, circa 1894. The brownstone Queen Anne-style residence with an attached jail features the original kitchen, dining room, parlor, and bedrooms with related artifacts. Public areas contain the jail cells, sheriff's office, and an 1890 judge's bench—complete with a witness stand and jury chairs.
URL: *www.exploringthenorth.com/newberry/histmuseum.html*
CONTACT: (989) 306-1860

Tahquamenon Logging Museum

ADDRESS: One mile north of Newberry on M-123, Newberry, MI 49868
ADMISSION: Contact site.
ACCESSIBILITY: Fully accessible.
DESCRIPTION: The museum provides information and artifacts depicting the early days of logging. Attractions include a log cook shack, the original Camp Germfask CCC building, Port Huron steam engine #6854, a log home, the original one-room Pratt Schoolhouse, a Goldthorpe logging truck, and a nature trail.
URL: *www.tahquamenonloggingmuseum.org*
CONTACT: (906) 293-3700

ONTONAGON

Ontonagon County Historical Society Museum

ADDRESS: 422 River St., Ontonagon, MI 49953
ADMISSION: Charge.
ACCESSIBILITY: Partially accessible.
DESCRIPTION: Visit our museum telling the story of Ontonagon County through curated displays of historical artifacts and archival materials, encouraging the preservation, study, and research of life in Ontonagon County. Also, tour the Ontonagon Lighthouse which is curated as if a family was still living there, circa 1915.
URL: *www.ontonagonmuseum.org*
CONTACT: ochs@jamadots.com • (906) 884-6165

PAINESDALE

Champion #4 Shaft House

ADDRESS: 42634 N Shaft Rd., Painesdale, MI 49955
ADMISSION: Free. Donations accepted.
ACCESSIBILITY: Fully accessible.
DESCRIPTION: Painesdale Mine and Shaft, Inc. works to preserve the oldest remaining shaft house in Copper Country—Champion #4 Shaft-Rockhouse. Visitors can experience the sights, sounds, smells, and the feel of mining as it once was. Along with the shaft house, there are numerous industrial buildings, railway equipment, and private homes related to the mining area on site.
URL: *www.painesdalemineshaft.com*
CONTACT: painesdalemine@gmail.com • (906) 369-5358

PHOENIX

Bammert Blacksmith Shop

ADDRESS: North of Phoenix, along M26 towards Eagle River, Phoenix, MI 49950
ADMISSION: Free. Donations accepted.
ACCESSIBILITY: Fully accessible.
DESCRIPTION: The Bammert Blacksmith Shop was built in the 1880s at the Cliff Mine location and moved to Phoenix in 1906. Amos Bammert built buggies, sleighs, and wagon wheels in this shop. Various tools of the blacksmith trade, including the original forge, are on display today.
URL: *www.keweenawhistory.org*
CONTACT: Contact via website. • (906) 289-4990

Phoenix Church and Museum

ADDRESS: 5581 US-41, Phoenix, MI 49950
ADMISSION: Free. Donations accepted.
ACCESSIBILITY: Contact site.
DESCRIPTION: Visit the Church of the Assumption in Phoenix, which held masses for mining families and their descendants for a century. Originally, this was St. Mary's Church, built in 1858. In 1899, the church was dismantled and reassembled in Phoenix. Although now deconsecrated, the church holds weddings and memorial services.
URL: *www.keweenawhistory.org*
CONTACT: Contact via website. • (906) 289-4990

PICKFORD

Pickford Area Historical Museum

ADDRESS: 175 E. Main St., Pickford, MI 49774
ADMISSION: Free. Donations accepted.
ACCESSIBILITY: Fully accessible.
DESCRIPTION: A National Register of Historic Places site, the museum constantly changes the exhibits while showcasing life in the area since 1877. Included in the collection are exhibits dealing with logging, farming, music, churches, schools, outdoor sports, and military, among others. Guests are invited to peruse the large genealogy section and the children's interactive hands-on area.
URL: *www.pickfordmuseum.org*
CONTACT: pickfordpassages@gmail.com • (906) 647-1372

REPUBLIC

Pascoe House Museum

ADDRESS: 183 Cedar St., Republic, MI 49879
ADMISSION: Contact site.
ACCESSIBILITY: Partially accessible.
DESCRIPTION: The Pascoe House, an 1800s house operated by the Republic Area Historical Society, contains changing exhibits that uncover the occupational, economic, social, and cultural history of the city of Republic. On display are farm and logging items, church and business history, mining artifacts, household items, family genealogies, photo albums, and old publications.
URL: *www.republicmichigan.com/historical-society*
CONTACT: owilliams3411@att.net • (906) 376-8827

ROCKLAND

Rockland Township Historical Museum

ADDRESS: 40 National Ave., Rockland, MI 49960
ADMISSION: Contact site.
ACCESSIBILITY: Fully accessible.
DESCRIPTION: The museum is dedicated to the history of Rockland Township's people, copper mines, and businesses, along with the first telephone system in the state of Michigan. Home settings include a kitchen, dining room, parlor, and bedroom. Mining, farming, school, and military displays are featured as well as photographs, newspapers, and documents. Genealogical research is also available.
URL: *www.ontonagonmuseum.org/partners-historic-sites*
CONTACT: ochs@jamadots.com • (906) 886-2821

RUDYARD

Rudyard Historical Society Museum

ADDRESS: 18725 S Mackinac Trl., Behind the Fire Deptment and Township offices, Rudyard, MI 49780
ADMISSION: Free. Donations accepted.
ACCESSIBILITY: Fully accessible.
DESCRIPTION: The society, which operates under township authority, was formed in 2005. Monthly meetings are held and are open to the public. We have published several historical books and have a little museum as well as a replica of a one-room schoolhouse made with authentic Rudyard bricks.
URL: *www.rudyardtownship.org*
CONTACT: 2ktreml@gmail.com • (906) 478-5041

SAULT STE. MARIE

Chippewa County Historical Society Museum

ADDRESS: 115 Ashmun, St. Sault Ste. Marie, MI 49783
ADMISSION: Contact site.
ACCESSIBILITY: Fully accessible.
DESCRIPTION: The museum is located in the 1889 building that originally housed the *Sault Ste. Marie News*, owned by Chase S. Osborn, the only governor elected from the Upper Peninsula. Exhibits include an American café, railroads, and other changing displays that cover the economic, social, and cultural history of Sault Ste. Marie, Chippewa County, and the Upper Peninsula.
URL: *www.cchsmi.com*
CONTACT: history@cchsmi.com • (906) 635-7082

SKANEE

Arvon Township Historical Society Museum

ADDRESS: 13510 Roland Lake Rd., Skanee, MI 49962
ADMISSION: Free. Donations accepted.
ACCESSIBILITY: Contact site.
DESCRIPTION: The museum was built in 1909 and was originally the parsonage for Zion Lutheran Church that is located across the road and celebrated 125 years in July 2017. The society maintains the house as close to the period as possible. There is a photo gallery of the early citizens as well as genealogies of those early families.
URL: *www.arvontownship.org/points-of-interest/historical-museum*
CONTACT: rebel45@up.net • (906) 524-4942

SOUTH RANGE

Copper Range Historical Museum

ADDRESS: 44 Trimountain Ave., South Range, MI 49963
ADMISSION: Free. Donations accepted.
ACCESSIBILITY: Contact site.
DESCRIPTION: Visitors will enjoy exhibits that help re-create the rich history of what life and work were like for miners, loggers, farmers, businesses, homemakers, and families, along with sports memorabilia, during the copper mining era. There's a 'what's-it' table where you may identify what the items are or recall your ancestors having it in their homes.
URL: *www.pasty.com/crhm*
CONTACT: copperrangehistoricalsociety@gmail.com • (906) 487-9412

ST. IGNACE

Father Marquette National Memorial

ADDRESS: 592 Boulevard Dr., St. Ignace, MI 49781
ADMISSION: Recreation Passport required.
ACCESSIBILITY: Fully accessible.
DESCRIPTION: The Father Marquette National Memorial tells the story of the French missionary-explorer who founded Sault Ste. Marie in 1668, St. Ignace in 1671 and explored the Mississippi River with Louis Jolliet in 1673. In addition to the memorial itself, the site features a short interpretive trail and views of the Mackinac Bridge. The site is part of the Michigan History Center's Museum System.
URL: *www.michigan.gov/marquettememorial*
CONTACT: mhcinfo@michigan.gov • (906) 643-8620

Fort de Buade Museum

ADDRESS: 334 North State St., St. Ignace, MI 49781
ADMISSION: Contact site.
ACCESSIBILITY: Partially accessible.
DESCRIPTION: On display are the Newberry Tablets. Other exhibits include a Native-American collection, which includes stone tools, everyday objects, baskets, ceremonial artifacts, headdresses, and regalia; dioramas depicting a voyageur with trade goods; a trading post; and a representation of Chief Satigo's lodge. The museum is operated by the Michilimackinac Historical Society.
URL: *www.michmackhs.org*
CONTACT: fortdebuademuseum@gmail.com • (906) 984-2234

VULCAN

Iron Mountain Iron Mine

ADDRESS: W4852 Hwy U.S. 2, Vulcan, MI 49892
ADMISSION: Charge.
ACCESSIBILITY: Partially accessible.
DESCRIPTION: Located nine miles east of Iron Mountain, the Iron Mountain Iron Mine keeps alive the heritage of the area's underground mining ancestors. The site provides guided underground mine tours by a train of the former east Vulcan mine, which produced more than 22 million tons of iron ore from 1870 to 1945.
URL: *www.ironmountainironmine.com*
CONTACT: Contact via website. • (906) 563-8077

WAKEFIELD

Wakefield Historical Society Museum

ADDRESS: 306 Sunday Lake St., Wakefield, MI 49968
ADMISSION: Free. Donations accepted.
ACCESSIBILITY: Contact site.
DESCRIPTION: With artifacts dating from 1884, the Wakefield Historical Society Museum features displays that include a mining room; a general store; a classroom; a doctor's office; Esther's closet, an exhibit of women's period clothing; and an area dedicated to the military service of the city's residents.
URL: *www.wakefieldmihistoricalsociety.org*
CONTACT: wakefieldmihistoricalsociety@gmail.com • (906) 224-1045

INDEX

C

D

E

F

G

H

I

J

K

L

M

N

O

P

Q

R

S

T

U

V

W

Y

Z

ABOUT HSM

Promoting Our State, Our Stories Since 1828

As the oldest cultural organization in Michigan and the official state historical society, the Historical Society of Michigan (HSM) provides programming, publications, awards, and assistance to entities and individuals of all ages across the state. The Society hosts three annual conferences, weekly history talks for general audiences, workshops, children's history programming, organizational support, and more. HSM also produces several history publications for a variety of audiences, including the statewide favorite, *Michigan History* magazine.

Committed to diversity and telling the stories of Michiganders, HSM is dedicated to bringing you the Great Lakes State's history—all in one place.

WHAT WE DO

- Host a membership program which connects individuals and families with Michigan stories, events, and organizations
- Publish *Michigan History* magazine, the largest statewide history magazine of its kind in the country
- Produce history publications for all ages—from grade school to academia—with our publications
- Host three annual conferences throughout the state for history buffs and local residents
- Present history lectures, workshops, and other events to anyone interested in Michigan history topics
- Connect hundreds of Michigan's local historical organizations with each other and with the public
- And more!

Get involved today by becoming a member, attending an event, or reading our publications!

Learn more about the Historical Society of Michigan
The Historical Society of Michigan hosts exciting events, programs, and more. Learn more at *hsmichigan.org*.